# Life Work Revolution

*How to Unplug from "The System,"
Find Your Purpose, and Thrive
Beyond the 9-5.*

## KASON MORRIS

# FOREWORD

In the midst of a demanding corporate career, I realized that the traditional definitions of success—titles, paychecks, and prestige—were not enough. Burnt out and underpaid, I knew I needed a change. This realization led to the birth of the Life-Work Revolution, a movement dedicated to helping professionals, especially those from underrepresented backgrounds, achieve true fulfillment by redefining success on their own terms.

The Life-Work Revolution is built on three core pillars: Internal Revolution, External Revolution, and Community Revolution. These pillars are designed to guide you through a comprehensive transformation that integrates personal growth, professional development, and community impact.

As a father, corporate executive, and entrepreneur, achieving life-work alignment and financial independence has been crucial for me. This journey has taught me that the best life and career are the ones you design, blending purpose, resilience, and community. This book aims to share these insights and provide a roadmap for your own life-work revolution.

We all crave freedom—the freedom to live the life we truly want, to move forward, and to achieve our full potential. Yet, many of us feel stuck, unable to break free from the constraints that hold us back. You can break free from the system and get off the struggle bus.

I emerged stronger through nearly two decades of personal and professional challenges, including significant setbacks and struggles. Each obstacle fueled my determination to climb the conventional ladder of success and eventually create workplaces where individuals could thrive and discover their authentic selves.

True success isn't about titles or status—it's about choices, well-being, purposeful growth, and impact.

## Unplugging from the System

A key aspect of the Life-Work Revolution is unplugging from the system. This involves reframing your narrative to understand that you are not defined by your title or work success. It's not about working hard to the bone but about beating the system by recognizing its constraints—the degree, the job, the debt, and the rat race—especially those imposed by systemic barriers on marginalized backgrounds.

Embracing a new life system and work where skills, experience, story, and network create leverage helps you navigate life and work on your terms. Detaching self-worth from fancy degrees or titles allows for healthy professional detachment, enabling you to see jobs as utilities and sponsors of your revolution and evolution.

Financial discipline is another lever for the freedom you seek. It's about using your professional acumen for income diversification, which underpins the external revolution through side hustles and gig culture, enabling you to always be in the driver's seat in your career and life 4.0 revolution.

This book shares principles and practices to help you create a life of purpose and fulfillment, becoming a revolutionary in your own right. You can achieve lasting transformation by integrating these principles into your daily life.

Are you ready to unlock the limitless possibilities that await you? I invite you to join me on this transformative journey. Embrace these timeless principles, and let them be the guiding light that leads you to a future where you don't just survive but thrive in and beyond the 9-5.

# TABLE OF CONTENTS

# INTRODUCTION
## Unplugging From The System

Welcome to the Life-Work Revolution. This journey represents a profound shift in defining success, particularly for leaders and executives of color from marginalized groups. Born from my own experiences navigating leadership while staying true to my identity, this system serves as a guiding light for those who have felt sidelined, underestimated, or confined by narrow corporate success definitions.

## Reframing the Narrative: Internal Shift

The first step in unplugging from the system is reframing your narrative. Traditional success metrics—titles, paychecks, and degrees—often fail to capture the true essence of personal and professional fulfillment. For many, especially those from marginalized backgrounds, the systemic barriers and societal expectations impose an additional layer of constraint. This book invites you to reclaim your story, redefine your success, and understand that your worth is not defined by external accolades but by your internal growth and resilience.

Research Insight: According to a study by Harvard Business Review, individuals who actively reshape their career narratives and focus on intrinsic motivations report higher levels of job satisfaction and personal well-being (HBR, 2023).

## Embracing a New System: Skills, Experience, Story, and Network

The Life-Work Revolution advocates embracing a new system where skills, experiences, stories, and networks create leverage. In

Career 4.0, your value is derived from your unique capabilities and the narrative you build around them. This shift allows you to navigate your career on your terms, moving fluidly between roles and industries as opportunities arise.

Research Insight: A McKinsey report highlights that skills-based hiring and internal talent marketplaces are becoming crucial for organizations to remain competitive in the digital age (McKinsey, 2022).

## Detaching Self-Worth from Titles and Certifications

A critical aspect of this revolution is detaching your self-worth from fancy titles or certifications. Healthy professional detachment enables you to view your job as a utility—a means to fuel your personal and professional growth—rather than a definitive measure of your worth. This perspective allows you to pursue roles and projects that align with your values and long-term goals without being constrained by conventional success metrics.

Research Insight: The American Psychological Association emphasizes the importance of professional detachment in preventing burnout and promoting long-term career sustainability (APA, 2021).

## Financial Discipline: Powering Legacy and Freedom

Part of the revolution involves cultivating financial discipline as a tool for legacy building and achieving freedom beyond the 9 to 5. You can enhance your financial stability and independence by leveraging your professional acumen to diversify income streams through side hustles or gig work. This approach is not about providing financial advice but shifting your mindset towards sustainable financial habits and compounding earnings for long-term freedom.

Research Insight: According to a report by the Financial Health Network, individuals who engage in multiple income-generating activities report higher levels of financial security and resilience (FHN, 2023).

## Your Journey Begins

Growing up in The Bronx, New York, I experienced firsthand the struggles and triumphs of striving for success against the odds. Like many of you, I worked tirelessly to climb the success ladder, achieving impressive titles and accolades. Yet, despite these achievements, I felt a persistent void. It wasn't until I faced my own breaking points—burnout, underpayment, and a messy divorce—that I realized true success isn't measured by titles or paychecks but by the joy, fulfillment, and balance we create.

Since then, I have emerged as a father of four beautiful daughters and a dedicated husband leading a bi-continental American and Ghanaian household and as a Managing Director and VP of Learning Development for both fast-growing startups and Fortune 500 companies. I have accomplished ten strategic promotions across five different industries, increased my salary tenfold, launched multiple business ventures using my skills, experiences, story brand and value networks as leverage, and discovered joy and fulfillment in my work, all thanks to embracing the concept of life-work design.

## Join the Life-Work Revolution

The Life-Work Revolution is about helping you create a life of purpose and fulfillment. This book will guide you through understanding and applying the core principles to your unique journey. Are you ready to begin? Join me in this transformative journey, embrace these timeless principles, and let them be the guiding light that leads you to a future where you don't just survive but thrive beyond the 9 to 5.

## You are About to Change Your Life:
## THIS IS MY GIFT TO YOU

## Scan the QR Code Above!

# Part 1:
## The Fundamentals - Understanding the Life-Work Revolution

For years, we've heard about 'work-life balance.' It's almost a mantra. The concept is so ingrained that people say, "I'm trying to establish a good work-life balance so I can spend time with my loved ones regularly." You might even say it's cultural. But have you ever felt something's missing? This concept implies that life must fit around work. In reality, you need a "life-work synergy," i.e., the belief that your well-being must be prioritized over everything else. Life-work synergy may not seem so different from work-life balance, but it has a much more significant impact.

Traditionally, humans were conditioned to view work as the most dominant part of life. The average employee works too hard to live their life fully. Before the pandemic, they followed a rigid 9-5 schedule. Every day was commuting, office hours, and commuting. There was very little room for anything else. Due to the classic 9-5 job structure, most employees had no say on where and when they worked. It left no room for flexibility. This and many other factors combined together to spark the Life-Work Revolution for me.

Thanks, in part, to the pandemic making work-from-home non-negotiable, many have realized that it is possible to function professionally in a home environment and thrive. As such, there's a sweeping embrace of life-word synergy, and many are ready to leave work-life balance behind. And you should be, too!

# LIFE-WORK SYNERGY

Relationship

Health

Personal
Growth

LIFE

SYNERGY

WORK

Achievements

Career

Professional
Growth

# Chapter 1:
## The Need for a Revolution

The Life-Work Revolution is a crucial shift, especially for marginalized group leaders and executives of color. Historical revolutions have transformed how we live and work, from the Industrial Revolution to the Digital Age. Today, we face a new change – a Life-Work Revolution prioritizing holistic success, personal fulfillment, and community impact. This revolution addresses marginalized professionals' unique challenges, offering a path to a more balanced and fulfilling life.

As an executive shaping the future of work and skills, and with nearly two decades of experience in corporate talent development and management consulting, I've witnessed firsthand the need for this revolution. My journey, particularly as a person of color navigating various corporate landscapes, industries, roles, and technological innovations, has equipped me with the insights necessary to lead this transformative movement.

## Historical Life-Work Revolutions

Historically, there have been pivotal moments when societies underwent significant transformations in how they approached life and work. Technological advancements, social changes, and economic shifts often drove these revolutions.

- **The Agricultural Revolution**

Early humans lived a hunter-gatherer lifestyle in the beginning. They foraged wild plants and hunted animals for food. Then, around 10,000 BCE, they experienced the first agricultural revolution. This was also referred to as the Neolithic Revolution.

The agricultural revolution marked the transition from nomadic hunter-gatherer societies to settled farming communities. It single-handedly initiated the development of human civilization in monumental ways.

Here's how it happened: As the Ice Age ended, the environment shifted to a milder and warmer climate. This allowed humans to settle in specific locations and start growing crops and raising animals. They grew crops like wheat, barley, and legumes and domesticated animals like sheep, goats, and cattle. The small gardens eventually turned into bigger farms.

The early humans were also able to invent crop rotation, plant and animal breeding, other cooperative labor techniques, and plows and irrigation systems. These tools and techniques allowed them to produce larger amounts of food, which, in turn, facilitated population growth.

Since farming required staying in a specific place, humans also created permanent settlements. The increase in food production enabled them to establish villages, towns, and eventually, cities – leading to the rise of civilizations worldwide. At the same time, there was enough time to engage in non-agricultural activities, such as trade, crafts, and governance.

**Impact**: The agricultural revolution changed human societies at the very core. It established the foundation for structured work, property ownership, and social hierarchies. Living in settled communities allowed humans to pursue other interests, including arts, architecture, and writing. They also introduced structured governance, law, and organized religion to manage the complexities of the new societies. This revolution laid the framework for the emergence of modern society, ultimately leading to the Industrial Revolution.

- **The Industrial Revolution**

The Industrial Revolution happened between the late 18th century and early 19th century. It was a transformative period where human societies experienced substantial changes in agriculture, manufacturing, mining, transportation, and technology. Naturally, the impact was significant. The industrial revolution in Britain from whence it spread to other parts of the world. It facilitated the shift from agrarian-based economies to industrial-based ones.

During this era, humans made major technological and social advancements. The steam engine, power loom, spinning jenny, and other machines were invented to increase production efficiency. Humans also moved from human and animal labor to water power, steam, and electricity. Also, iron and steel production improved, allowing them to produce cheaper and stronger infrastructure. All of these progresses dramatically increased production capabilities.

**Impact**: The industrial revolution led to significant economic transformations, urbanization, employment opportunities, and major social changes. Production was centralized, allowing factories to hire large numbers of workers, increasing output. Plenty of people moved to the new cities for work. This also contributed to the rise of capitalism as local markets expanded internationally. Private ownership, investment, and profit were of particular interest to people.

Everything in life has pros and cons, so it should be no surprise that the industrial revolution brought about challenges such as labor exploitation and environmental degradation.

Factory work was especially harsh and dangerous. Wages were low, and working conditions were abysmal. The working class responded to this by establishing labor unions and movements to advocate for their rights. Unfortunately, the industrial era further widened the gap between the rich and the poor.

Furthermore, this era increased the use of natural resources, such as coal, iron, and timber, disregarding the environment. Air and water pollution were incredibly high, further degrading the environment and creating many health hazards.

Still, the Industrial Revolution was so profound that it redefined every aspect of society and facilitated unprecedented economic growth, technological advancement, and social transformation.

- **The Information Revolution**

There is no bigger factor for the modern global economy than the information revolution, also known as the Digital Revolution. It began in the late 20th century and centers around the rise of computers, the internet, and digital communication technologies.

Think of the information revolution as a massive shift in how humans handle data and knowledge. In the past, humans relied on physical books, newspapers, and mail to communicate. As a result, communication was slow, and information was hard to come by. The Information Revolution changed all of this. Thanks to the rise of digital technology, it has become incredibly easy to access information anytime, anywhere. This has revolutionized learning, working, communicating, and entertaining ourselves.

**Impact**: This revolution changed how we access, process, and share information, leading to the rise of the knowledge economy. It created new industries, transformed existing ones, and altered the nature of work by emphasizing intellectual labor over physical labor. But there are downsides. The information revolution has also brought about misinformation, privacy concerns, and digital divides.

Despite the progress we've undergone due to these historical revolutions, humans face unique challenges in modern society that require a new approach to life and work. Let me show you what I mean.

Current Challenges and the Need for a New Approach

As you can see, how society has evolved over the centuries is vast. Several challenges have presented for modern society as part of globalization, industrialization, and digitization. We cannot overcome these current challenges with a 20th-century mindset. That is why we need an approach. Here are some of these challenges:

- **Technological Disruption**

A technological disruption occurs when new technology transforms how businesses, industries, and consumers operate. In this modern business landscape, disruptive technology has become pervasive, constantly reshaping industries and the job market. This disruption fundamentally alters how humans and businesses operate.

For example, advances in artificial intelligence, automation, and robotics are transforming industries at an unprecedented pace. They require new skill sets, thus making many traditional job roles obsolete. As a result, there is a skills gap between the current workforce and the rapidly evolving job market. According to a McKinsey report, up to 375 million workers (14% of the global workforce) may need to switch occupational categories by 2030. Thus, workers must continually adapt to new technologies.

- **Economic Inequality**

Every time society undergoes a revolution, the gap between the poor and the rich widens. This is especially true in recent decades as the standard of living constantly increases due to agriculture, healthcare, and technology developments. The problem is that wages for the low-to-moderate working class have failed to go up with the rising living costs.

Individuals at the mid-to-lower end of the income spectrum are at high risk of losing their jobs to new, disruptive technology. They are also less likely to have the resources necessary to train and upskill for higher-paying jobs.

Economic inequality leads to disparities in access to education, healthcare, and opportunities. This is particularly pronounced for marginalized groups, who are concentrated in lower-paying job roles and often face systemic barriers to success. Without a new approach, many of today's employees won't have the necessary skills to remain employed or seek new opportunities in the job market.

## • Work-Life Imbalance

Achieving a balance between your life and work is necessary to find more satisfaction, feel more motivated, and spend quality time with your loved ones. Sadly, the demands of modern work often encroach on personal life, leading to stress, burnout, and a decline in overall well-being.

Work-life imbalance is the inability of professionals to establish boundaries between work life and personal life, leading to high-stress levels and decreased productivity. Achieving a healthy work-life balance in a hyper-connected, always-on world is increasingly difficult.

Many employees have trouble drawing a line in the sand regarding their needs and those of their employers. According to the American Institute of Stress, job stress is the primary source of stress for American adults and has escalated progressively over the past few decades. Increased stress levels can have long-term, negative effects on your physical and mental health.

## • Environmental Sustainability

Our natural environment provides many of the resources used in everyday life. We use them to grow crops, mine for metals and minerals, harvest wood, and obtain water. Contrary to what many believe, the Earth has finite land, water, wildlife, etc. Therefore, it's important to have environmental sustainability to ensure these and other natural resources are around for future generations who will need them for survival.

Urgent global issues, such as climate change and environmental degradation, have made this difficult. As such, we must adopt a more sustainable approach to living and working to protect this planet for future generations. This includes adopting greener practices and reducing our carbon footprint.

To further illustrate why we need a new approach to address these modern challenges, I'll share a few personal stories about different individuals I know.

## Illustrative Stories and Examples

- **Story 1:**

Reggie, an international marketing executive of Ghanaian descent, found his role evolving rapidly due to AI and automation. Instead of resisting change, he embraced new technologies, taking courses to upskill himself in data analytics and AI. This proactive approach secured his job and positioned him as a valuable asset in his organization.

Reggie's commitment to learning paid off. He could now analyze customer data more efficiently, predict market trends, and create targeted marketing strategies. His team looked to him for guidance on integrating AI tools, and management noticed his growth. This led to new opportunities and responsibilities.

**Lesson**: Embracing technological advancements and continuously updating skills can turn potential threats into opportunities.

**Key Question**: What technological advancements can you embrace to stay ahead in your field?

- **Story 2:**

Sarah, a first-generation Latina tech executive, faced significant barriers in her career due to economic disparities. These obstacles made it difficult for her to access the same opportunities as her peers. However, she didn't let these barriers stop her. Through mentorship programs and community support, she accessed resources and opportunities that helped her rise to leadership positions. Her journey wasn't easy, but she persevered, knowing that her success could pave the way for others like her. Today, Sarah is dedicated to giving back. She mentors others from similar backgrounds, guiding them through the same challenges she once faced. By sharing her experiences and knowledge, Sarah helps the next generation of tech leaders navigate and overcome these barriers.

**Lesson**: Building supportive networks and giving back can help mitigate the effects of economic inequality.

**Key Question**: How can you leverage mentorship and community support to overcome economic barriers?

- **Story 3:**

Brooks, a mid-level manager of African American lineage, found himself constantly stressed and burned out due to an overwhelming workload. It seemed like no matter how hard he tried, he couldn't catch a break.

Then, he decided to make a change. By implementing life-work synergy strategies, Brooks set clear boundaries between his work and personal life. He made a point to prioritize his well-being, making time for exercise, hobbies, and family. These changes didn't happen overnight, but they made a significant impact. Brooks noticed his stress levels decreasing and his overall quality of life improving. Thanks to them, he achieved a healthier life-work balance.

**Lesson**: Prioritizing well-being and setting boundaries are essential for achieving a life-work balance.

**Key Question**: What steps can you take to prioritize your well-being and set clear boundaries?

- **Story 4:**

Emily, an engineer of Colombian heritage, incorporated sustainable practices into her work by advocating for green technologies and reducing waste in her projects. Her efforts benefited the environment and positioned her as a leader in sustainability within her industry.

Emily's journey began with a simple idea: to make her engineering projects more eco-friendly. She tirelessly researched and implemented green technologies, ensuring each project minimized environmental impact. From using renewable energy sources to promoting recycling and waste reduction, Emily's commitment to sustainability is evident in every aspect of her work.

By sharing her knowledge and advocating for green practices, Emily has inspired others to follow suit, creating a ripple effect of positive change.

**Lesson**: Adopting sustainable practices can create a positive environmental impact and enhance professional reputation.

**Essential Question**: What sustainable practices can you adopt to contribute to environmental sustainability in your work?

## The Need for a Life-Work Revolution

Given the challenges of modern society discussed above, a new Life-Work Revolution is essential. This revolution aims to redefine success, particularly for marginalized groups, by promoting life-work synergy, sustainable practices, and inclusive growth.

Society's measure of success has always been based on material wealth, job titles, and professional accomplishments. The average person may associate success with these metrics, but the dictionary says it's "the accomplishment of an aim or purpose." From this, it's clear that success can be unique to each individual. As a matter of fact, it has little to do with money or power in most cases.

With the Life-Work Revolution, holistic well-being is central to defining and perceiving success. Key markers include mental and physical health, work-life balance, and personal happiness. The goal is to find fulfillment and contentment beyond your work in all aspects of life.

Being able to control where and when you work is another key marker of success in this revolution. It comes with the freedom to dictate your schedule and work environment, which means you can better integrate your work with your personal life. That is how I achieved a more balanced and fulfilling lifestyle.

You must seek meaningful work that aligns with your personal values and passions. The revolution entails looking beyond personal gain to focus on your impact on others and your environment. It emphasizes engaging in purposeful work, donating to causes you care about, and making a positive difference in any way you can. It also encourages you to embrace lifelong learning and growth by constantly acquiring new skills and evolving your career. You must be adaptable and resilient in this rapidly changing society.

Healthy interpersonal relationships are crucial to success in the Life-Work Revolution. Whether spending time with loved ones, making friends, or nurturing a support network, you need quality relationships for overall happiness and satisfaction in work and life.

Like me, you can also make sustainable living a part of your journey. By this, I mean making environmentally conscious choices, supporting ethical business, and following a lifestyle that reduces your carbon footprint. Don't just view success in personal terms but in your contributions to a sustainable future.

Ultimately, success in the Life-Work Revolution is about harmonizing your personal life and work so seamlessly that neither overshadows the other. It broadens the definition of success to include every vital aspect of life. This makes it not only attainable but sustainable and enriching.

Here are a few tips to start embracing this redefinition of success:

## Reframe and Take Back the Narrative

Many of us, particularly those from marginalized backgrounds, have been socialized to measure success by material wealth, job titles, and professional accomplishments. We've been caught in a rat race, endlessly trying to meet societal expectations. It's time we made a change. You are so much more than your work success or salary figures. And that's why the first step in the Life-Work Revolution is to reframe and take back your narrative.

**Action**: Learn to view yourself as a unique individual defined by a wealth of skills, experiences, healthy relationships, and, more importantly, optimal well-being. To do this, you must shift to a mindset that prioritizes the things that truly matter to you. Conforming to societal expectations of success can be misleading. Your personal aspirations – those things that truly mean something to you – are what matters.

- Think about what matters most to you outside of work. These things will help identify your core values so that you can prioritize them in everyday life.

- Create goals based on the values you've identified. Your life goals and values should always align.

For example, consider an individual who has been climbing the corporate ladder for years. This person has a prestigious title but has had to sacrifice personal passions and relationships along the way. As a result, they feel unfulfilled in life.

You don't want to be this person. So, by reframing your narrative, you can learn to value your hobbies, family relationships, and community involvement just as much as your work success. Reframing and taking back your narrative will help others recognize what you truly value.

**Key Question**: How can you reframe your narrative to focus on what truly matters to you?

### Embrace a New System of Life and Work

To further shift your mindset from traditional success markers, you must embrace a new life and work system. This new system emphasizes skills, experience, story, and network. That way, you can create leverage to navigate life and work on your terms. The objective is to empower you to take charge and make decisions that align with your values and goals.

This new system also emphasizes what you can actually do over your degree. Skills and practical experience are more valuable to employers than a specific credential. You need them to deliver results and adapt quickly.

**Action**: Develop a dynamic career strategy. Your strategy should involve investing in continuous learning and skills development. For instance, you might take new courses regularly, attend workshops, and earn certifications in your field. This will help enhance your skills and keep you updated.

Networking should be a key part of your strategy. Consider joining professional groups, attending industry events, and connecting with peers on social media platforms. A personal brand reflecting your skills, values, and experiences will also make a remarkable difference. This approach will help you stay adaptable and prepared for whatever comes your way.

**Key Question**: What steps can you take to develop a career strategy that aligns with your values and aspirations?

- **Detach Self-Worth from Titles and Degrees**

If you truly want to redefine success for yourself, you must practice healthy professional detachment. This means viewing your job as a tool for growth and revolution rather than a measure of your worth. Understand that your value isn't tied to your degrees or professional titles. Instead, it's about your capabilities and impact.

**Action**: Be proactive about detaching your worth and value from external markers like titles or degrees. Focus on your skills and ability to learn and adapt.

- Regularly reflect on skills and accomplishments that are unrelated to your job title. Write them down and come up with ways to improve.

- Ask the people in your life for feedback on strengths and areas of impact. Use the feedback to understand yourself better.

- Pursue activities and projects outside of your job role.

Take someone who has always prided themselves on being a "manager." If this person moves to a new role without a similar title or better, they might feel insecure since their self-perception hinges on their professional title. That's why you must appreciate your true value beyond titles and credentials.

**Key Question**: How can you detach your self-worth from external markers and focus on your true value?

- **Financial Discipline as a Tool for Freedom**

Without financial discipline and income diversification, freedom beyond the classic 9 to 5 is impossible. If you leverage your professional skills, you can create additional revenue streams through side hustles and gig work. Doing this can enhance your financial status and subsequently lead to complete financial freedom.

**Action**: Adopt financial discipline. Create a budget, save, and invest wisely. Explore multiple income streams to ensure you aren't entirely dependent on your main income for financial insecurity. Without financial constraints, you can freely pursue your interests and passions.

- Create a budget and stick to it consistently.

- Identify skills that can be monetized outside of your primary job.

- Research investment opportunities and invest in stocks, bonds, real estate, and cryptocurrencies to build long-term wealth.

Let's say you have a full-time job. In that case, you might start a freelance consulting business on the side. The extra income can be incredibly helpful in paying off debts faster, saving for future goals, or transitioning to full-time self-employment if that is your dream.

**Key Question**: What financial strategies can you implement to achieve greater freedom and stability?

Follow these tips to get started on the path to redefining what success means to you as you embrace the Life-Work Revolution.

### Summing It Up

We've seen significant progress through historical revolutions, but today's challenges call for a new approach. The Life-Work Revolution promotes holistic success, sustainable practices, and inclusive growth. Start by reframing your narrative, embracing new systems, detaching self-worth from titles, and practicing financial discipline. Ready to transform your life and work? The next chapter will guide you further.

## Key Takeaways

- Historical life-work revolutions have shaped how we live and work.

- Current challenges such as technological disruption, economic inequality, work-life imbalance, and environmental sustainability require a new approach.

- The Life-Work Revolution promotes holistic success, life-work synergy, sustainable practices, and inclusive growth.

Reframing the narrative, embracing a new system, detaching self-worth from titles, and adopting financial discipline are critical components of the revolution.

### Looking Ahead

Congratulations on beginning this journey through the Life-Work Revolution. As we continue, the next chapter will delve into the core principles of the Life-Work Revolution, providing a foundation for transforming your life and work. Together, we will explore strategies to create a fulfilling, balanced life that honors your unique identity and aspirations.

# Chapter 2:
## Core Principles of the Life-Work Revolution

The Life-Work Revolution is built on several core principles that can guide you in creating a life that aligns with your values and aspirations. These principles provide a structured approach to building the new life you want. Think of them like the key ingredients in the recipe for your desired lifestyle. Just as a great meal requires a balanced combination of spices, flavors, and textures, you need a blend of these principles to create a fulfilling life. Each adds a unique spice and flavor to your life so that you can satiate your deepest dreams and aspirations.

The core principles are connected to the three core revolution pillars: the Internal Revolution, the External Revolution, and the Community Revolution. These pillars provide a framework for understanding and applying the core principles in different aspects of your life. They are dynamic, adaptable, and designed to help you thrive in a world increasingly characterized by complexity and uncertainty.

Before we discuss the seven core principles, I'll briefly explain what the three pillars entail.

**Internal Revolution**

The Internal Revolution is about personal growth, mindset, and well-being. This pillar encourages you to look inward and reflect on your beliefs, attitudes, and behaviors. It's about understanding yourself better, recognizing your strengths and areas for improvement, and committing to ongoing personal development. When you focus on your internal world, you cultivate resilience, emotional intelligence, and a positive mindset – all essential for overcoming life's challenges.

## External Revolution

The External Revolution involves adapting to career changes, skill development, and leveraging technology. As I've reiterated a few times, staying stagnant isn't an option in today's fast-paced world. As such, this pillar centers on the importance of being proactive in your career, continuously learning, and adapting to remain relevant and fulfilled. Whether mastering new technologies, developing in-demand skills, or shifting career paths, the External Revolution is about embracing change and using it as an opportunity for growth.

## Community Revolution

Lastly, the Community Revolution emphasizes building and leveraging networks, creating impact, and establishing community support. Humans are inherently social creatures; we thrive when we're part of a supportive network. This pillar encourages you to build strong, meaningful relationships with mutual support and growth. Engaging with your community helps to create a network of peers, allies, and mentors who can provide guidance, support, and opportunities.

Based on these pillars, the following are the 7 core principles of the Life-Work Revolution.

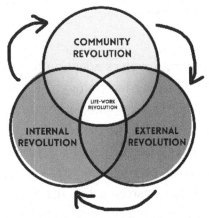

## Core Principle 1: Life-Work Synergy

Life-work synergy is all about integrating your personal and professional goals to make your life more balanced and fulfilling. You must ensure that what you do for work not only fits into your life but also enriches it. Imagine a situation where your job is not just a way to earn a paycheck but actually adds value to your personal life. This means that your work should support your overall well-being and align with your personal values. In turn, your personal satisfaction should enhance your effectiveness and happiness at work.

Studies have shown that balancing work and life leads to higher job satisfaction, lower stress levels, and improved overall well-being (American Psychological Association)(career-pathways-research…). So, this isn't just feel-good advice; it's backed by research.

**Example**: Early in my career, I recognized the importance of aligning my work with my values. This realization led me to prioritize roles and opportunities that allowed me to make a meaningful impact, personally and professionally. For instance, since I value family time, I make sure my work schedule allows me to be present for important moments with my lovely wife and kids.

**Exercise**: Take some time to reflect on your current work and life activities. Start by listing what you do each day – professionally and personally. Once you have a clear picture, think about where there might be opportunities to align your personal values with your professional goals.

For instance, ask yourself: Do aspects of your job resonate with what you care about most? If you find discrepancies, it's time to explore how to create more synergy between your work and personal life. Once you know what to do, focus on incremental adjustments instead of overhauling everything at once. For instance, you could start incorporating more of your personal interests into your work.

Creating life-work synergy will help you achieve personal and professional fulfillment in the long term.

## Core Principle 2: Developing Durable Skills

Durable skills remain valuable over time, regardless of changes in technology or industry trends. These include critical thinking, emotional intelligence, and adaptability.

According to the World Economic Forum, durable skills like critical thinking, adaptability, and emotional intelligence are increasingly valued in the modern job market. (World Economic Forum, Future of Jobs Report 2023).

- Critical thinking is about analyzing information and making well-reasoned decisions. It helps you solve problems effectively, no matter the situation.
- Emotional intelligence involves understanding and managing your emotions while being sensitive to others' feelings. You need this skill to build strong relationships and work well with people from all backgrounds.

- Adaptability is the ability to adjust to new conditions and easily handle change. As industries evolve and new technologies emerge, adaptability ensures you can stay ahead and thrive.

Unlike technical skills, which tend to become obsolete, durable skills stand the test of time. They aren't just nice-to-haves – they're critical for long-term success. You need them to maneuver career shifts, manage stress, and work collaboratively with others. Honing these skills prepares you not just for the present but for the future as well.

**Example**: Developing durable skills enabled me to navigate multiple career transitions successfully. I have leveraged this principle to transition from various roles, always focusing on alignment with my core values and long-term vision.

**Exercise**: Start by making a comprehensive list of your current skills. Include everything from technical abilities to soft skills like communication or teamwork. Once you have your list, take some time to categorize these skills into two groups: durable and perishable.

Note that perishable skills are specific and can become outdated as technology or industry standards evolve. For example, proficiency in a specific software version or knowledge of a particular method might be crucial now but could become less relevant in the future. Once you have your list, strengthen your durable skills through continuous learning and practice.

The goal is not just to maintain your skills but to keep them sharp and relevant.

## Core Principle 3: Cultivating a Growth Mindset

You may or may not be familiar with the concept of a growth mindset. A growth mindset believes abilities and intelligence can be developed through education and hard work because they are not fixed traits. This mindset nurtures resilience by shifting the focus from innate talent to effort and learning. You learn to see challenges as opportunities to grow rather than obstacles to avoid.

With this mindset, you realize that failure doesn't reflect your abilities or skills. Instead of feeling defeated by setbacks, you'll approach them with curiosity and determination. A growth mindset makes you eager to learn and improve, which, in turn, empowers you to embrace new experiences and persist through adversity.

Research from Stanford University emphasizes that a growth mindset contributes significantly to career adaptability and success." (Dweck, Carol S., Mindset: The New Psychology of Success).

Carol Dweck's research on the growth mindset shows that individuals who believe their talents can be developed (through hard work, good strategies, and input from others) tend to achieve more than those with a more fixed mindset(career-pathways-research…).

**Example**: Brooks embraces a growth mindset by continuously seeking new learning opportunities, such as online courses and professional development workshops. This mindset helps him overcome challenges and stay competitive in his field.

**Exercise**: Think about a recent challenge or setback you faced. It could be a demanding project at work, a personal goal that didn't quite pan out, or any situation where things didn't go as planned. How did you react initially? Did you feel discouraged, frustrated, or even defeated?

Now, imagine how adopting a growth mindset might have changed your perspective. Start by writing down your thoughts on the challenge you faced. Ask yourself how a growth mindset could help you handle similar situations more effectively in the future. For example, consider what you can learn from the experience instead of focusing on what went wrong and how you can apply these lessons moving forward.

Having a growth mindset will positively influence your Life-Work Revolution process.

## Core Principle 4: Prioritizing Well-being

When I say "prioritizing your well-being," I talk about self-care. This means taking care of your physical, mental, and emotional health. Think about it this way: if you don't care for yourself, everything else in your life becomes harder to manage. When your body feels good, your mind is clearer, and your emotions are balanced – which makes you better equipped to handle the demands of work and life. Self-care is essential for avoiding burnout and achieving sustainable success.

If you don't prioritize your well-being through self-care, you risk exhausting yourself. And that can lead to decreased productivity, poor decision-making, and overall dissatisfaction. On the other hand, when you make your health a priority, you're more likely to achieve your goals and enjoy the journey.

According to the World Health Organization, workplace well-being initiatives can significantly reduce health risks, improve employee productivity, and lower absenteeism(career-pathways-research...).

**Example**: Emily incorporates well-being into her daily routine by practicing mindfulness, exercising regularly, and setting boundaries between work and personal time. This approach helps her maintain high performance without sacrificing her health.

**Exercise**: Assess your current well-being practices. Start by looking at the basics: Are you getting enough sleep each night? Sleep is crucial for physical and mental health, so if you're often tired, adjusting your sleep schedule might be worth adjusting. Next, consider your exercise routine. Regular physical activity can boost

34

mood, improve energy levels, and reduce stress. Even a short daily walk can make a difference if you're not currently exercising. Don't forget about mindfulness. Practicing mindfulness can help you manage stress and stay focused. Simple techniques like deep breathing or short meditation sessions can be very effective.

Once you've identified areas where you can improve, set small, achievable goals; for instance, if you aim to get better sleep, try setting a consistent bedtime. If exercise is a goal, commit to a 15-minute workout each day. Start small and gradually build on these changes. This way, you can make steady progress without feeling overwhelmed.

Remember, this journey will be practically impossible without this core principle. Self-care is non-negotiable.

## Core Principle 5: Building Community

A healthy community comprises people willing to provide mutual support and guidance to one another. Building a community involves creating and nurturing relationships that promote individual and collective growth. When you invest in your community, you're not just making connections but building a network of allies who can help you succeed.

Think about it. A strong community provides valuable resources, advice, opportunities or someone to lean on during tough times. Having mentors can guide you through your career and personal challenges. People with experience in your field can offer insights and experiences that can save you time and effort. Plus, being part of a community gives you a sense of belonging, which is crucial for your well-being.

Harvard Business Review notes that strong professional networks are correlated with career advancement and higher job satisfaction." (Harvard Business Review, Networking That Works).

**Example**: Reggie continues to build his professional community by participating in industry groups and networking events. These connections provide him with support and opportunities for collaboration.

**Exercise**: Review your current network and identify key individuals who can offer support and mentorship. Who in your circle inspires you, provides valuable advice, or challenges you to grow? These are the connections worth nurturing. Reach out to these people and seek ways to strengthen your relationships with them. A simple message or a coffee chat can go a long way. Ask about their experiences, share your goals, and find common ground.

Building a strong network is about more than what others can do for you; it also has everything to do with what you can do for people. The objective is to help each other succeed, especially if you're from marginalized groups.

Focus on creating meaningful, reciprocal relationships that will benefit both parties in the long run.

## Core Principle 6: Embracing Adaptability

What does it mean to be adaptable? Adaptability is the ability to adjust to new conditions and environmental changes. It would be best if you had it to survive and thrive in this rapidly changing world. It's all about being flexible and open to change.

Things constantly shift, whether in your career, technology or even social dynamics. Being adaptable means you can handle these changes without getting overwhelmed. Consider the last time you had to learn a new skill quickly or adjust to a sudden change at work. How did you handle it? If you adapted well, you probably stayed calm, figured out what needed to be done, and took action. This ability to adjust and move forward is what makes adaptability so important.

By the way, being adaptable isn't just about reacting to change; it's also about anticipating it. It means being proactive, seeking out new experiences, and constantly learning. You're not stuck in old ways of thinking when you're adaptable. Instead, you're ready to pivot and embrace new ideas and methods. If you can adapt, you can stay relevant, make the most of new opportunities, and maintain your well-being amid the chaos.

McKinsey Global Institute reports that career adaptability and skills-based transitions are critical for future job security." (McKinsey Global Institute, Jobs Lost, Jobs Gained).

**Example**: Sarah's adaptability allows her to navigate the dynamic landscape of the tech industry. She continuously advances her career by staying flexible and open to new opportunities.

**Exercise**: Think about a recent change or unexpected event in your life. How did you handle it? Maybe it was a job change, a move to a new city, or a sudden shift in your personal life. Consider your response – did you embrace or resist the change? What could you have done differently to adapt better?

Part of embracing adaptability is being open to and learning from new experiences. Next time you face an unexpected event, try to approach it with curiosity and a willingness to learn. Ask yourself: What can I gain from this experience? How can this change help me grow personally and professionally? You can also practice adaptability by taking small, everyday actions. Try stepping out of your comfort zone regularly. Take on a new project at work, learn a new skill, or meet new people.

The more you expose yourself to new experiences, the more adaptable you'll become.

## Core Principle 7: Creating Impact

This principle involves using your skills and resources to impact your community and industry positively. You must take what you're good at and the resources you have and use them to bring about positive change in any way you can. This is how to build a lasting legacy.

All of the skills you've honed over the years – whether it's your knack for solving problems, your ability to connect with people, or your expertise in a particular field – can help address real-world issues or support a cause you care about.

When you make a positive difference, you're not just helping others but also creating a sense of fulfillment for yourself. You're contributing to something bigger than yourself, which can be incredibly rewarding. Plus, you're building something that will outlast your career and possibly even your lifetime.

Research shows that individuals who feel their work positively impacts others are more engaged and motivated (Harvard Business Review)(career-pathways-research…).

**Example**: Emily focuses on creating impact by leading sustainability initiatives in her engineering projects. Her efforts contribute to environmental conservation and inspire others to adopt sustainable practices.

**Exercise**: Identify areas where you can impact your personal or professional life. First, examine the various aspects of your life. Where do you feel a pull to make a difference? Is it in your career where you could mentor a junior colleague, or perhaps in your community where you could volunteer for a local cause? Identifying these areas is the first step to creating a meaningful impact.

Set specific, actionable goals once you've pinpointed where you want to make a difference. If your goal is to make a positive impact at work, you might aim to lead a new project, improve a process, or support your team members' professional development. In your personal life, your goals could include starting a community garden, organizing a neighborhood clean-up, or simply being there more for your friends and family.

Now, it's crucial to track your progress. How do you ensure you're moving towards your goals? Regular check-ins can help. Create a simple plan to review your progress weekly or monthly. Ask yourself, "What steps have I taken toward my goal? What has worked well? What could I improve?" This review keeps you accountable and helps you stay on track.

Creating impact isn't just about grand gestures. Instead, it's about the cumulative effect of your efforts. It's about being intentional with your actions and thinking about how you can use your strengths and skills to improve the world daily.

### Summing It Up

The seven core principles of the Life-Work Revolution—Life-Work Synergy, Developing Durable Skills, Cultivating a Growth Mindset, Prioritizing Well-being, Building Community, Embracing Adaptability, and Creating Impact—provide a foundation for transforming your life and work. By incorporating these principles, you can navigate modern challenges purposely and with resilience.

# Key Takeaways

- Life-Work Synergy: Integrate personal and professional goals for a balanced life.
- Developing Durable Skills: Focus on skills that remain valuable over time.
- Cultivating a Growth Mindset: Embrace the belief that abilities can be developed.

- Prioritizing Well-being: Take care of your physical, mental, and emotional health.
- Building Community: Create and nurture supportive relationships.
- Embracing Adaptability: Adjust to new conditions and changes.
- Creating Impact: Use your skills to make a positive difference.

**Looking Ahead**

In the next chapter, we will dive deep into your journey. I will provide a framework to help you start your personal Life-Work Revolution and guide you through the process step by step. Get ready to learn how to align your daily actions with your long-term goals, embrace the principles of the Life-Work Revolution, and build the life you deserve and desire!

# Chapter 3:
## Your Journey Begins

Every journey begins with a single step. The Life-Work Revolution is no different. Before we begin your journey, let me share my personal story detailing how I applied the core principles of the Life-Work Revolution to navigate multiple career transitions and achieve a work-life balance successfully. This will help you realize the exact ways in which this journey will transform your life and career.

## My Personal Story

It was very early in my career that I had a pivotal experience that shaped my career path in ways that I would never have imagined. I remember sitting in a café, listening intently as my mentor shared a personal story about their own career journey. They spoke about learning to pursue work that reflected what truly mattered to them a decade after being in the industry transformed their personal and professional lives. They also told me about their regret for not doing it sooner. For my mentor, even though it seemed late at the time, that decision eventually led to greater fulfillment and success. This conversation was a turning point for me.

This invaluable insight opened my eyes to how much I wanted (and needed) to align my work with my personal values. Realizing this alignment's significance, I started seeking roles, skills, and opportunities that resonated with the things I truly value in life. I embraced the core principles of the Life-Work Revolution and let them guide me in successfully navigating multiple career transitions across different industries.

For example, when I transitioned from marketing to a leadership role in Management Consulting, I focused on building strategic thinking and communication skills. This wasn't just about shifting industries but about finding ways to make a meaningful impact.

In another instance, I emphasized adaptability and collaboration when moving into SaaS. I took on projects that allowed me to lead teams through complex changes. I ensured we aligned with the company's mission and values. These roles demanded a high level of adaptability, which I was able to deliver.

Similarly, when I ventured into the Insurance and Life Sciences sectors, I leveraged my leadership development and strategic planning skills. Each career transition was guided by my commitment to align my work with my core values and long-term vision. This approach facilitated a smoother transition and helped me stay true to my purpose. This alone made each role more fulfilling than the previous one. It has been instrumental in my journey to becoming a strategic global Future of Work executive and skills-based organization (SBO) advisor.

What does this mean for you?

**Reflecting on Your Journey**

To begin your own life-work revolution, it's essential to reflect on your journey so far. Understanding where you have been and what you have learned will provide valuable insights for your future path. Taking the time to think about your experiences can help you make better decisions moving forward.

**Exercise**

**1. What are your core values, and how have they influenced your career choices?**

Consider what principles matter most to you. Are you driven by creativity, integrity, or perhaps helping others? Reflect on how these values have shaped the jobs you've taken and the career paths you've pursued.

## 2. What skills and experiences have you gained that you consider durable and valuable?

Think about the abilities you've developed that stand the test of time, like critical thinking, problem-solving, or communication. These are your durable skills. Identify specific experiences where these skills have been crucial.

## 3. How have you handled challenges and setbacks in your career?

Look back at the obstacles you've faced. How did you overcome them? Did you learn new skills, seek help from mentors, or find new ways to approach problems? Understanding your resilience strategies can be incredibly empowering.

## 4. What are your long-term personal and professional goals?

Dream a little. Where do you see yourself in five, ten, or twenty years? Consider both your personal life and your career. What do you want to achieve, and what steps can you start taking now to get there?

Answering these questions will give a clearer picture of your strengths, values, and goals. This self-awareness is the first step in aligning your life and work, ensuring both bring you satisfaction and purpose.

## Setting Intentions

Setting clear intentions is a crucial step in your life-work revolution. Intentions guide your actions and decisions, helping you stay aligned with your values and goals. When you know what you want to achieve, making choices supporting those outcomes is easier.

Take Sarah, for instance. She decided to focus on leadership and diversity initiatives. She knew exactly where to direct her energy because she set clear intentions. This clarity allowed her to pursue roles and projects that matched her goals. As a result, Sarah transitioned into a leadership role at a tech startup, where she could drive meaningful change. Her intentions didn't just guide her; they made it possible for her to make a real impact.

The question is, how can you apply this to your own life? Writing down your intentions can be a powerful tool. It makes your goals tangible and gives you a roadmap to follow. Here's a simple exercise to help you get started:

**Exercise: Writing Down Your Intentions**

**1. Personal Growth**: What areas do you want to develop or improve in your personal life? Think about your passions and interests. Do you want to read more, learn a new skill, or improve your health? Maybe you want to become more mindful or better at managing stress. Write down specific areas you want to work on.

**2. Professional Development**: What skills or experiences do you want to gain in your career? Consider where you want to be in your career in the next few years. Do you need to learn a new technology, improve your leadership skills, or gain experience in a different aspect of your industry? List the skills and experiences that will help you reach your professional goals.

**3. Community Engagement**: How do you want to contribute to your community or industry? Think about the causes you care about and how you can make a difference. Do you want to volunteer, mentor, or lead an initiative at work? Maybe you want to join a professional organization or start a community project. Write down the ways you can engage with and support your community.

Setting clear intentions in these areas is the key to creating a blueprint for what's to come. Your intentions will guide your daily decisions and ensure you stay on track with your personal and professional aspirations. They help you focus on what truly matters to you so that you can say no to distractions and yes to opportunities that align with your goals.

44

Keep in mind that intentions aren't set in stone. They can evolve as you grow and as your circumstances change. You only have to review them regularly and adjust as needed. That's how to stay focused on what matters most to you.

## Framework for Your Life-Work Revolution

As you begin this journey, you'll need a framework to keep you aligned with your short-term and long-term goals. This framework will provide clarity, focus, and direction. More importantly, it will keep you consistent, accountable, and efficient as you pursue your goals. I love having one because it allows flexibility, decreases stress, and keeps me motivated, no matter the odds. Ultimately, having a framework will help you navigate the life-work revolution purposely, aligning your actions with your core values. Ready to start?

Here's what your framework might look like:

**1. Identify Your Core Values**

Start by identifying your core values. These will guide your decisions and actions.

- Personal Integrity: What does honesty and authenticity mean to you?
- Professional Excellence: How do you define high-quality work?
- Work-Life Balance: What does a healthy balance look like for you?
- Continuous Learning: How do you prioritize personal and professional growth?

**2. Set Clear Goals**

Outline your short-term and long-term goals. Make sure they align with your core values.

- **Short-Term Goals (Next 6-12 Months):**

45

- ➤ Complete a professional certification.
- ➤ Enhance your writing portfolio with diverse content.
- ➤ Establish a consistent work routine.
- **Long-Term Goals (Next 2-5 Years):**
  - ➤ Publish a book or a series of articles.
  - ➤ Build a strong network within your industry.
  - ➤ Achieve a significant work-life balance milestone.

### 3. Create an Action Plan

Break down your goals into actionable steps. This makes them more manageable and less overwhelming.

- **Daily Actions:**
  - ➤ Dedicate 1-2 hours to writing or research.
  - ➤ Practice mindfulness or a short exercise routine.
  - ➤ Check and adjust your to-do list.
- **Weekly Actions:**
  - ➤ Network with at least one professional contact.
  - ➤ Attend a webinar or read an industry-related article.
  - ➤ Consider your progress and adjust your plans if needed.
- **Monthly Actions:**
  - ➤ Evaluate your goals and achievements.
  - ➤ Set new short-term goals if necessary.
  - ➤ Plan a break or a small reward for your efforts.

### 4. Stay Flexible and Adapt

Life and work are dynamic. Be prepared to adjust your plans as needed.

- Conduct a weekly review of your progress.
- Reflect monthly on what's working and what's not.

- Be open to changing your strategies if they don't align with your goals and values.

### 5. Build a Support System

Surround yourself with people who support your goals and values.

- **Mentors and Peers:**
  - ➢ Seek advice from experienced professionals.
  - ➢ Collaborate with peers who share similar goals.
- **Accountability Partners:**
  - ➢ Find someone who can hold you accountable for your commitments.
  - ➢ Share your progress and challenges with them regularly.

### Summing It Up

Starting your life-work revolution involves reflecting on your journey, setting clear intentions, and developing a framework for continuous growth. With these strategies, you can remain aligned with your goals and values as you embrace the Life-Work Revolution. Your journey is just as important as the destination, so remember.

# Key Takeaways

- Reflecting on your journey provides valuable insights for your future path.
- Setting clear intentions guides your actions and decisions.
- Developing a framework helps you stay aligned with your values and goals.
- Continuous learning and building a strong network are crucial for growth and resilience.

### Looking Ahead

This chapter has been all about exploring the basics of beginning your revolution. Now, it's time to dive into the more practical aspects of this journey. In the second part of this book, we will look at the Internal Revolution across three different chapters. We will focus specifically on how you can achieve life-work synergy, develop durable skills, and cultivate a growth mindset. I may have shared some fundamental tips in the book's first part, but these coming chapters will provide more information and practical advice. Prepare to transform your inner world and set the foundation for a successful life-work revolution.

# Part 2:
## The Internal Revolution - Transforming Your Inner World

Are you stuck in an endless loop in your personal and professional life? You're on autopilot, going through life but not living. This is where an internal revolution comes into play. It's all about transforming your inner world to create a more fulfilling life and career.

As previously explained in Chapter Two, an internal revolution is akin to a deep, personal upheaval. It's a process of reevaluating your beliefs, habits, and patterns. This transformation is key to greater self-awareness, purpose, and, ultimately, a more meaningful existence. But why do you need this revolution within yourself?

**Aligning Values and Actions**

The first reason an internal revolution is essential is its role in aligning personal values with professional actions. An internal revolution necessitates a deep examination of your core values and beliefs. When you gain clarity on what truly matters to you, making career choices and taking daily actions that align with those values becomes easier. Without this internal alignment, your external achievements may feel hollow and unsatisfying, undermining the overall goal of a life-work revolution.

**Overcoming Limiting Beliefs**

Another critical aspect of the internal revolution is how it helps us challenge and overcome limiting beliefs. Whether you know it or not, internalized doubts and negative self-beliefs may hold you back. For instance, you may believe you aren't capable or deserving of success. An internal revolution involves confronting and replacing these limiting beliefs with more positive and beneficial thoughts. This is how you open the door to new possibilities and opportunities.

**Enhancing Self-Awareness**

Self-awareness is one of the most crucial components of personal and professional growth. The process of an internal revolution initiates a deeper understanding of your strengths, weaknesses, motivations, and desires. This enhanced self-awareness will enable you to make more informed decisions regarding your career and personal life. A clearer sense of your identity and goals will allow you to create a life-balance that is both sustainable and satisfying. But without this self-awareness, you may struggle to juggle your career and personal life effectively, defeating the life-work revolution's purpose.

**Nurturing Authenticity**

Authenticity is a necessity for a fulfilling and successful life. An internal revolution pushes you to live more authentically by aligning your actions with your true self. This enhances personal satisfaction and attracts opportunities and relationships that resonate with your authentic identity. In the life-work revolution, living authentically will allow you to pursue careers and personal activities that coincide with your true passions.

Ultimately, an internal revolution plays a key role in shaping a clear vision for the future. With the insight you gain, you develop a coherent and motivating vision for your life and career. This provides direction and purpose and guides you through the process of integrating your personal and professional goals.

In essence, the internal revolution is a fundamental prerequisite for a successful life-work revolution. The core principles make it an indispensable element of the broader revolution. To get started, we will explore the first principle of the internal life-work revolution: life and work synergy.

# Chapter 4:
## Embracing Life-Work Synergy

Do you remember what I said about work-life balance being a modern myth? That's right – it's an elusive ideal we've been conditioned to chase after. You may think the key to happiness is achieving a perfect equilibrium between work and life, but this constant striving will only lead to frustration and burnout. Therefore, it's time to challenge this traditional notion and introduce a more holistic and achievable model: Life-Work Synergy.

Imagine life and work as two sides of a coin. You can't have one without the other; each side needs the other to shine. If life is the head, guiding you with your values and passions, then work is the tail, pushing you forward with purpose and direction.

Think about how a coin spins. Both sides blur into one seamless entity in motion, working together to keep the momentum going. That's what life-work synergy is all about. It's not just about balancing your job and personal life but making them work together harmoniously. When you align your work with your personal values and passions, everything feels more effortless. As I've said before in earlier chapters, you won't just be working; you will thrive.

Have you ever noticed how a well-balanced coin lands perfectly? It's the same with life and work. When they're in sync, you're more productive and happier. You can give your best in both areas because neither is draining the energy needed for the other.

According to studies reported by the American Psychological Association, individuals with high levels of life-work synergy report greater job satisfaction, reduced stress, and improved overall well-being.

I have experienced this as I learned early on to make life-work synergy a core part of my career. As such, I sought roles and opportunities where I could make a meaningful impact without compromising my growth and well-being.

The problem with the traditional views on life-work balance is that they are limiting. Here's what I mean by this.

## Traditional Views and Their Limitations

Our current, traditional view on work-life balance promotes a zero-sum game where we consider our daily lives and careers as opposing forces. As a person of color, this perspective can be especially restrictive due to our distinct systemic barriers.

Research by McKinsey & Company highlights these challenges, including higher unemployment rates and significant underrepresentation in high-wage industries. However, if you redefine those outdated concepts and expectations, you can follow a life-work model where your personal life and career complement instead of competing with each other.

Unlike the traditional work-life perspective, life-work synergy focuses on reordering perspectives to put personal growth, aspirations, and well-being at the center of your professional life. It's how I have achieved a masterful shift from "work-life" to "lifework." Integrating my personal identity into my career pathways has enabled me to follow a prosperous, fulfilling professional journey that respects and utilizes the unique strengths and perspectives I bring to the table.

## Living by SEASONS: A Framework for Synergy

We all know that life isn't a straight line. It ebbs and flows, much like the changing seasons. Recognizing and adapting to life's seasons is crucial for sustainable success. Just as nature cycles, our careers and personal lives have their own rhythms. Tuning into these rhythms can help us better manage our focus and energy on each aspect of our lives at different times. Embracing these seasons helps us become more dynamic and responsive to the challenges and opportunities that come our way.

The SEASONS framework:

## SEASONS ACRONYM

| | Start with intention | Embrace growth | Act with purpose | Sustain momentum | Optimize and reflect | Navigate transitions | Share and impact |
|---|---|---|---|---|---|---|---|
| | | | | | | | |
| | | | | | | | |
| | | | | | | | |

**1. Synergy**: Think about how your personal and professional goals can work together. When they do, life feels more balanced and fulfilling, doesn't it? So, how can you blend your work ambitions with your personal passions?

**2. Energy**: Do you ever feel like you're running on empty? Managing your energy levels is crucial. Staying productive is much easier when you keep an eye on how much energy you're expending and ensure you aren't burning out. How can you start listening to your body and mind, ensuring you're recharged and ready to take on tasks?

**3. Alignment**: Do your daily actions align with your core values and long-term goals? It's important to ensure what you're doing today supports where you want to be tomorrow. Start making sure that your daily activities reflect what matters to you.

**4. Support**: We all need a support system. Who do you have in your corner, and how can you strengthen those connections? Surround

54

yourself with colleagues, friends, and family who lift you. They're your cheerleaders when times are tough and when you succeed.

**5. Opportunity**: Always be on the lookout for growth and development opportunities. Seizing these moments can propel you forward. And when there are no opportunities, prepare your own. What new skills can you learn, or what projects can you undertake to push your boundaries?

**6. Navigation**: Life is full of challenges and transitions, which require resilience to navigate effectively. How adaptable are you? How do you handle setbacks? What strategies help you stay flexible and optimistic? The better you can navigate changes, the smoother your journey will be.

**7. Sustainability**: Focus on long-term sustainability in your work and personal life. This means making choices that support your ongoing health and happiness. Are your current habits and routines setting you up for a sustainable future? What can you do today to ensure your personal and professional life remains fulfilling and successful over time?

If you adopt and live by the SEASONS framework, you will be able to handle the dynamic nature of life better. The key is to be proactive, adaptable, and mindful of the different phases you go through. So, take the first step to embrace your seasons and find synergy now.

Let's examine examples of how other professionals have applied the SEASONS framework.

**REGGIE:**

• **Synergy**: Reggie finds a way to blend his marketing work with his tech passion by choosing projects that combine both fields. For instance, he recently led a new app launch campaign requiring expertise in both areas.

- **Energy**: He keeps his energy levels up by making time for regular exercise and hobbies. Every morning, he goes for a run, and on weekends, he enjoys coding small projects for fun.
- **Alignment**: Reggie ensures his career choices align with his long-term goal of becoming a leader in tech-driven marketing. Last year, he accepted a role at a startup that perfectly matched his vision for the future.
- **Support**: He constantly updates his network of mentors and peers who offer guidance and support. Reggie has just joined a tech-marketing mastermind group that meets monthly.
- **Opportunity**: Reggie always looks for learning and growth opportunities, like enrolling in tech courses. He recently completed a course on AI in marketing, which has already proven useful in his current projects.
- **Navigation**: He easily handles career transitions, using his adaptable skills to move forward. When his company underwent restructuring, Reggie seamlessly transitioned into a new role that better suited his evolving skills.
- **Sustainability**: Reggie is committed to a sustainable career path that allows for continuous growth without burning out. He practices time management techniques and unplugging from work during weekends to recharge.

**SARAH:**

- **Synergy**: Sarah leads various diversity initiatives at her company due to her passion. She aims to create a more inclusive workplace. For example, she recently spearheaded a program to mentor underrepresented employees, offering them guidance and support.
- **Energy**: Sarah practices mindfulness and takes regular breaks throughout her day to keep her energy up. These small pauses help her stay focused and refreshed.
- **Alignment**: Sarah's commitment to inclusion isn't just talk; it's in everything she does. When she notices a lack of diverse voices in

meetings, she actively encourages different perspectives to be heard. She believes that actions speak louder than words.

- **Support**: She connects with like-minded professionals and mentors who share her passion for diversity. They provide advice, support, and sometimes, just a listening ear when she needs it.
- **Opportunity**: Sarah is always looking for opportunities to share her knowledge. She frequently speaks at conferences and leads workshops on diversity, where she discusses her experiences and insights with others eager to learn.
- **Navigation**: She navigates the challenges of her new role with resilience and a growth mindset. When a project doesn't go as planned, she views it as a learning opportunity for the next project.
- **Sustainability**: Sarah focuses on sustainable practices by setting realistic goals and maintaining work-life synergy. This ensures she doesn't burn out and can continue contributing effectively to her mission of creating inclusive workplaces.

## BROOKS:

- **Synergy**: Brooks juggles his job and personal life using flexible work arrangements. For example, he often works from home on Fridays, allowing him to spend more time with his family.
- **Energy**: He keeps his energy up by focusing on activities that recharge him. He spends evenings with his family, playing games or watching movies together.
- **Alignment**: Brooks ensures his job matches his personal values. Flexibility and family time are non-negotiable, so he seeks roles that honor these priorities.
- **Support**: He has a support system at work. Brooks collaborates with colleagues who respect his work-life boundaries, like not scheduling meetings after 5 PM.
- **Opportunity**: Brooks looks for flexible projects that align with his interests. Recently, he joined a team that allows him to work remotely and focus on subjects he's passionate about.

- **Navigation**: He manages his job demands by setting clear boundaries. Brooks keeps a strict 9-to-5 schedule and uses productivity tools to manage his tasks efficiently.
- **Sustainability**: Brooks aims for sustainable work-life integration. He knows it's key to his long-term well-being, so he ensures he has enough time for his family and himself, making adjustments as needed.

**Creating a Life-Work Synergy System for Your SEASONS**

Here's a life-work synergy system I use to Implement SEASONS. Feel free to adapt it to suit your own needs:

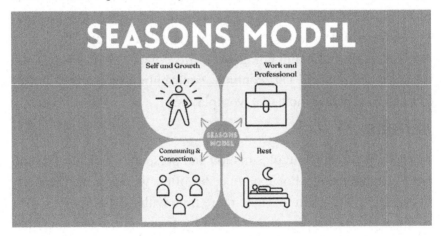

- **5 a.m. to 9 a.m. - Self and Growth**: Start your day with personal development. Engage in exercise, meditation, or skill-building activities that set a positive tone for the day. Maybe you enjoy a morning run, a yoga session, or a good book. I usually spend this time meditating and learning something new.
- **9 a.m. to 5 p.m. - Work and Business**: Engage deeply in professional tasks and business. Use the energy and insights from the morning to enhance productivity and creativity. This is the time to tackle challenging projects, meetings, and strategic planning. I focus on my current project and client meetings during these hours.

- **5 p.m. to 9 p.m. - Family and Connections**: Reconnect with family and community in the evening. Prioritize quality time with loved ones, social activities, and community engagement. This is essential for emotional support and personal fulfillment. I love having dinner with my family and catching up with friends during this period.

- **Sleep – Renewal and Reset**: Ensure you get quality rest to rejuvenate and prepare for the next day. Establish a consistent sleep routine to ensure you wake up refreshed and ready to take on new challenges. I aim for at least seven hours of sleep each night.

Depending on your unique needs and circumstances, this framework can be adapted to different times and scales – daily, weekly, monthly, or even quarterly. The key takeaway? Even if one segment doesn't go as planned, the others help you stay energized and adaptable.

## Micro-Exercise: Applying the SEASONS Framework and system

Let's make this practical. Here's a micro-exercise to help you apply the SEASONS framework to your life:

**1. Pick a Focus**: Choose one area of the SEASON's framework and system that you want to improve or integrate into your daily routine (e.g., self-growth, work, and business, family and connections, or sleep).

**2. Set Your Intentions**: Write down clear, measurable intentions for this area (e.g., meditating for 10 minutes every morning, dedicating two hours of undistracted time to family each evening).

**3. Make It Personal**: Reflect on the emotional benefits you'd gain from achieving these intentions and write a few sentences about it (e.g., feeling more centered and calmer, fostering stronger family bonds).

**4. Start Small**: Plan the first four weeks with micro-goals designed to get you part-way toward your big goal. Make these micro-goals easy and achievable.

**5. Track Your Progress**: Keep a journal or use an app to track your progress. Note what works, what doesn't, and any adjustments you must make.

**6. Reflect and Adjust**: At the end of four weeks, assess your progress. Reflect on what you've learned and adjust your goals as needed. Celebrate your achievements and set new micro-goals for the next four weeks.

According to recent research from the World Economic Forum, blending our personal and professional lives can lead to greater job satisfaction and productivity. This approach is especially valuable for leaders of color and marginalized groups who often face unique pressures. For instance, flexible work hours and remote work options can make a big difference. Companies that embrace these practices often see increased employee engagement and lower turnover rates.

Consider how companies like Google and Salesforce have implemented these strategies. Google's flexible work schedules and remote work policies have boosted employee morale and retention. Similarly, Salesforce's commitment to work-life balance has improved job satisfaction and fostered a more inclusive environment. By supporting Life-Work Synergy, businesses help employees manage their responsibilities more effectively and create a more positive workplace.

**Summing It Up**

Life-work synergy is about integrating your personal and professional goals to create a more fulfilling life. You can achieve life-work synergy by aligning your values, adopting flexible work arrangements, incorporating mindfulness practices, and committing to continuous learning. With the tips and strategies shared in this chapter, you are well on your way to doing this and creating a more fulfilling life and career.

## Key Takeaways

- Life-work synergy involves creating an integration between work and personal life priorities.
- Aligning your professional goals with personal values and routines is crucial for achieving life-work synergy.
- Flexible work arrangements, mindfulness practices, and continuous learning are key components of life-work synergy.
- Setting clear boundaries, prioritizing well-being, fostering strong relationships, and regular reflection are essential practices for maintaining life-work synergy.

### Looking Ahead

Now that we've explored the concept of life-work synergy, it's time to progress into the second principle of the Internal Revolution: Developing durable skills. The next chapter will take you through a step-by-step of building transferable and future-ready skills to provide you with a strong foundation for long-term success. Let's get into it.

# Chapter 5:
## Developing Durable Skills

A few years ago, I found myself in a jam. I juggled multiple projects and quickly shifted my approach to keep up with changing demands. It was a bombardment of deadlines and unexpected challenges. Thankfully, I had a solid set of durable skills developed over the years. These skills allowed me to adapt and thrive under the pressure of those projects.

Think of durable skills as a well-maintained toolbox and perishable skills as a bag of groceries. With its hammer, screwdriver, and pliers, your toolbox can be used for years to tackle various projects. It's always ready, no matter what task comes your way. These durable skills – like problem-solving, communication, and critical thinking – remain valuable and adapt to different situations over time.

On the other hand, perishable skills are like groceries that have an expiration date. If you stock up on fresh produce, it's great while it lasts, but eventually, it needs to be replaced. As you've learned, perishable skills include specific software knowledge or techniques that might become outdated as technology advances. They're useful for a certain period but need regular updating or replacement to stay relevant.

So, while keeping your "toolbox" of durable skills sharp is crucial, remember to refresh your "grocery list" of perishable skills as needed. While perishable skills are important for the specific tasks you tackle, durable skills provide a strong foundation for ongoing success. They don't just help you handle what's in front of you; they equip you to handle whatever comes next.

## Understanding Durable Skills

Durable skills, sometimes called transferable or soft skills, are essential traits that make us adaptable and effective in various roles and industries. These include empathy, the ability to adjust to new situations, a solid understanding of business principles (business acumen), and a knack for working well with others. Other key skills are data and analytics, an appreciation for diversity, equity, and inclusion (DEI), and digital and social media proficiency. Additionally, skills in systems thinking, ongoing personal development, and the ability to personalize and prioritize tasks are crucial.

What's great about these durable skills is their timelessness. As I said before, unlike technical skills that might become outdated as technology evolves, these abilities stay relevant and valuable no matter where your career takes you.

Research backs this up. According to the World Economic Forum, skills like complex problem-solving, critical thinking, and creativity will be incredibly important in the future job market. These durable skills will help us maneuver the increasingly complex work environments we face today. So, focusing on developing these skills can be a smart move for your career's future.

## Key Durable Skills

There are core, durable skills that are valuable no matter what industry, field, or role. These skills help you excel in your current position and prepare you for future challenges. Here's a closer look at these essential skills, how they can be applied, and ways to improve them.

**1. Empathy – Understanding and sharing the feelings of others.**

Empathy is putting yourself in someone else's shoes to understand and share their feelings. It's not just about feeling sorry for someone;

you have to genuinely grasp what they're experiencing and respond in a way that acknowledges their emotions. It is a compelling way to connect and build strong relationships with people. This makes empathy a crucial skill in life and any workplace.

**Example**: Take Emily, for instance. Her high level of empathy allows her to connect deeply with her colleagues and team members. This skill helps her build strong, trusting relationships, making her a natural leader others look to for guidance and support.

**Exercise**: To develop your empathy, start by practicing active listening. When conversing, focus on truly understanding the other person's perspective rather than just waiting for your turn to speak.

## 2. Adaptability – Adjusting to new conditions and challenges with ease.

Adaptability is how easily you adjust to new conditions and challenges. It's about being flexible and open to change rather than sticking rigidly to your old ways. Today's professional landscape makes this skill more important than ever. It can help you handle unexpected changes and new challenges effectively. This, in turn, can make you a valuable asset to any organization.

**Example**: Sarah showcased her adaptability when transitioning from a traditional corporate role to a leadership position in a tech startup. Her ability to learn quickly and embrace change made her a valuable asset to her new firm.

**Exercise**: Consider a recent change in your professional life. How did you handle it? Focus on areas where being adaptable would have helped even more. Then, experiment with different strategies to improve your adaptability for future changes. Perhaps you can try taking on a project you've never done or learn a brand-new skill.

### 3. Business Acumen – A deep understanding of the business, its goals, and its strategy.

When you hear "business acumen," it means a deep understanding of how a business operates, including its goals, strategy, and how different roles contribute to its success. It's about seeing the big picture and knowing how different parts of the business fit together. Strong business understanding allows you to make decisions that drive the organization forward and contribute to strategic planning and execution.

**Example**: Reggie is a great example of someone with strong business acumen. He uses this to make informed decisions that support his organization's objectives. His deep understanding helps him contribute effectively to strategic planning and execution.

**Exercise**: Take time to study your organization's business model, goals, and strategies. Understand how your role fits into the larger picture and consider ways to enhance your impact. This might involve learning more about the industry, analyzing market trends, or seeking mentorship from senior leaders.


### 4. Collaboration – Working effectively with others to achieve common goals.

How well can you work with others to achieve a common goal? If you can, that makes collaboration one of your durable skills. Collaboration is about being a team player and knowing how to bring out the best in others. It involves clear communication, empathy, active listening, and working together towards a shared objective. Effective collaboration enhances teamwork, improves productivity, and creates a more cohesive work environment.

**Example**: Brooks excels at collaboration. His ability to convey ideas clearly and listen attentively helps him work well with colleagues and clients, boosting teamwork and productivity.

**Exercise**: Engage in team-based projects and focus on building collaborative relationships. Practice transparent communication and active listening during team interactions. See how these skills can improve your teamwork.


## 5. Data and Analytics – The ability to interpret and draw insights from data.

In the age of information, being able to interpret and draw insights from data is invaluable. This skill helps in making data-driven decisions. It's about understanding trends, making informed decisions, and using data to support strategic planning.

**Example**: Emily's use of data and analytics is a great example. She applies her skills to support data-driven decision-making in her projects. Her ability to analyze data helps her identify trends and make informed choices that drive project success.

**Exercise**: Improve your data literacy by taking courses or workshops on data analysis. Practice analyzing data sets relevant to your work and draw actionable insights from them. This will help you learn to use data to drive decisions and strategies.


## 6. Diversity, Equity, and Inclusion (DEI) – Understanding and promoting DEI principles.

DEI is about creating a workplace where everyone feels valued and included, regardless of background. It's about understanding and promoting diversity, equity, and inclusion principles. Embracing DEI contributes to a workplace culture where diverse perspectives are valued, and everyone has the opportunity to succeed.

**Example**: Sarah leads diversity initiatives in her organization. She has created an inclusive workplace culture that values diverse perspectives and encourages everyone to contribute their unique ideas. This commitment not only enhances employee satisfaction but also drives innovation and success.

**Exercise**: Educate yourself on DEI principles and practices. Advocate for inclusivity in your workplace and participate in or lead DEI initiatives. Reflect on how you can create a more inclusive and equitable work environment.

## 7. Digital and Social Skills – Proficiency in using digital tools and social media.

Being adept with digital tools and social media is crucial in this digital age. Digital and social skills involve proficiently using digital tools and social media effectively. It helps you stay connected, engage with your audience, and enhance your professional presence online.

**Example**: Reggie leverages digital tools and social media platforms effectively to enhance communication and engagement in his role.

**Exercise**: Familiarize yourself with the latest digital tools and social media trends. Use these tools to enhance your communication and professional presence online and stay updated on emerging technologies and trends to maintain your digital edge.

## 8. Systems Thinking – Understanding how different parts of the organization interact and influence each other.

Systems thinking sees how different parts of the organization interact and influence each other. It's about understanding the bigger picture and how changes in one area can impact others. You need this skill to identify and solve complex problems because it helps factor in the interconnectedness of various organizational components.

**Example**: Brooks applies systems thinking to solve complex problems at his company. By considering how his decisions impact various departments, he ensures that solutions are effective and sustainable.

**Exercise**: Study the interconnections within your organization. Reflect on how changes in one area can impact others. Practice holistic problem-solving approaches to improve your systems thinking skills.

### 9. Continuous Development – A commitment to ongoing learning and growth.

Continuous development is a commitment to ongoing learning and growth. It involves actively seeking opportunities to enhance your skills and knowledge. This skill ensures you remain relevant and up-to-date in a constantly evolving world. It helps you stay competitive and adaptable in your career.

**Example**: Emily's commitment to continuous development is evident through her engagement in workshops and courses. This dedication helps her keep her skills current and adapt to new challenges and opportunities.

**Exercise**: Identify areas for professional and personal growth. Set learning goals and pursue opportunities for continuous development through courses, workshops, and mentorship. Regularly assess your skills and seek feedback to guide your growth.

### 10. Personalization and Prioritization – Tailoring approaches to meet individual needs and prioritizing tasks effectively.

Personalization is tailoring your approaches to meet individual needs, while prioritization is managing your tasks effectively. Both are about understanding what's most important and focusing on them. They help to manage your workload efficiently and meet individual and team needs, which enhances productivity and job satisfaction.

**Example**: Reggie's ability to personalize his management approach helps him address the unique needs of his team members. This not only boosts productivity but also increases job satisfaction within his team.

**Exercise**: Reflect on your current task management strategies. Identify ways to personalize your approach to meet your and your colleagues' needs better. Practice effective prioritization to enhance productivity and achieve your goals more efficiently.

Hone these durable skills, and you will be equipped to thrive in any role or field. Each skill contributes to your overall effectiveness and success. Start by focusing on one or two areas for improvement and gradually incorporate them into your daily work. You'll find that not only will these skills enhance your current performance, but they'll also set you up for long-term success.

### Summing It Up

Developing durable skills is essential for long-term career success and adaptability. You can enhance your durable skills and stay competitive in a rapidly changing work environment by focusing on continuous learning, embracing challenges, seeking feedback, and practicing regularly. So, take the time to develop and refine these skills – your future self will thank you!

## Key Takeaways

- Durable skills remain valuable over time and are crucial for long-term career success.

- Empathy, adaptability, business acumen, collaboration, data and analytics, DEI, digital and social skills, systems thinking, continuous development, and personalization and prioritization are key durable skills.
- Continuous learning, embracing challenges, seeking feedback, and regular practice are essential for developing durable skills.

**Looking Ahead**

With a strong foundation of identified durable skills, we must continue our journey through the Internal Revolution by cultivating a growth mindset. In the next chapter, we will explore cultivating a growth mindset. This mindset will help you embrace challenges, learn from feedback, and persist in facing setbacks, further enhancing your personal and professional growth.

# Don't Forget to Claim Your Gift from
# Kason Morris:

## Scan the QR Code!

# Chapter 6:
## Cultivating a Growth Mindset

There's a common misconception in the corporate world that one must have what it takes. Anything can be learned and improved if one is willing to do the work. This is the entire basis of the concept of a growth mindset.

A growth mindset is a belief that abilities and intelligence can be developed through dedication and hard work, and it is one of the most invaluable assets any professional can have. Someone with a growth mindset believes their abilities, skills, and intelligence aren't set in stone.

They are confident that with work, they can improve any aspect of themselves over time. As a result, people with a growth mindset are typically resilient, with a love of learning and the ability to embrace challenges as opportunities for growth.

In contrast, someone with a fixed mindset believes that abilities and intelligence are static traits that cannot be significantly changed. Consequently, they avoid challenges, give up easily, see effort as fruitless, ignore useful feedback, and feel threatened by others' successes. They view failures as reflections of their inherent limitations.

Imagine your mind as a garden. A growth mindset is like a garden where you constantly plant new seeds, water them, and pull out weeds. You know that with patience and care, your garden will flourish with various flowers and plants.

On the other hand, a fixed mindset is like a garden where you plant a few seeds and then leave them be, assuming they will either grow or not, without any intervention. You believe whatever blooms or doesn't bloom is out of your control. There's no room for change or improvement, just acceptance of what is.

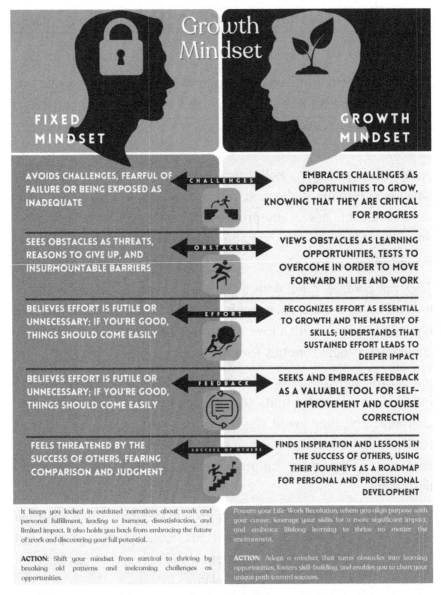

From this, you can see that cultivating a growth mindset is essential for personal and professional development. You must overcome obstacles and achieve long-term success.

# The Fundamentals of a Growth Mindset

Carol S. Dweck, a psychologist and professor at Stanford University, introduced the concept of a growth versus fixed mindset. Her research on mindset has had a significant impact on education and personal development.

Dweck's work suggests adopting a growth mindset can lead to greater motivation and achievement. It's about shifting your perspective from "I can't do this" to "I can't do this yet."

Have you ever caught yourself thinking you just aren't good at something? That's the fixed mindset talking. But what if you approached it with a growth mindset instead? How might that change your approach to learning and personal development? It's worth considering, don't you think?

Through extensive research and experiments, Carol Dweck supported her premise about growth versus fixed mindsets. She conducted numerous studies in educational settings. One famous study involved giving students a series of puzzles to solve. After some initial success, they were given much harder puzzles designed to be challenging. Students with a growth mindset viewed these challenges as opportunities to learn, while those with a fixed mindset quickly became discouraged and performed worse over time.

Another involved experimenting with different types of feedback. In one study, students were praised for their intelligence ("You must be smart at this") or their effort ("You must have worked really hard"). Those praised for effort were more likely to embrace challenges and persist in the face of difficulty, demonstrating a growth mindset. In contrast, those praised for intelligence tended to avoid challenges and were more likely to give up when faced with obstacles, reflecting a fixed mindset.

Dweck and her colleagues conducted long-term studies following students over several years. They found that students who believed they could improve their intelligence through hard work (a growth mindset) consistently outperformed those who believed their intelligence was fixed. This held true across different age groups and academic subjects.

They also cited neuroscience research showing that the brain can grow and change in response to effort and learning. This concept, known as neuroplasticity, supports the idea that abilities and intelligence are not static but can be developed.

So, a growth mindset's benefits are rooted in science and research. What are these benefits?

## The Importance of a Growth Mindset

Let's examine the benefits of a growth mindset before diving into the examples and exercises.

### 1. Embracing Challenges

A growth mindset encourages you to see challenges as opportunities rather than obstacles. When you face a tough situation, instead of feeling overwhelmed, you feel excited to tackle it and learn from the experience.

### 2. Learning from Criticism

With a growth mindset, criticism is not seen as a personal attack but as constructive feedback. You understand that feedback is a tool for improvement, allowing you to enhance your skills and performance. This openness to learning helps you grow continuously and improve at what you do.

### 3. Persisting in the Face of Setbacks

Setbacks are inevitable, but a growth mindset helps you view them as temporary and surmountable. Instead of giving up, you analyze what went wrong, learn from the experience, and try again. This persistence is crucial for achieving long-term success and overcoming obstacles.

**4. Seeing Effort as a Path to Mastery**

A growth mindset values effort as an essential part of the learning process. You recognize that putting in time and hard work leads to improvement and mastery of skills. This dedication to continuous learning and improvement can significantly advance your career and personal goals.

Considering these benefits, you can see the difference a growth mindset can make in your personal and professional life.

## Developing a Growth Mindset

The good news is that even if you don't have a growth mindset right now, it is possible to develop a growth mindset. Based on Carol Dweck's research, you can shift your mindset from fixed to growth through awareness and intentional effort. This transformation is supported by neuroscience, which shows that the brain can grow and change with effort and learning, reinforcing the idea that abilities are not fixed but can be developed over time.

Here are practical steps for developing a growth mindset:

**1. Embrace the Power of "Yet"**

The word "yet" holds a surprising amount of power. It's a small word, but it can create a big shift in your mindset. When you say, "I can't do this," it sounds definitive and final. It implies that your ability is fixed and there's no room for improvement. On the other hand, saying, "I can't do this yet," opens up possibilities. It suggests that while you might not be able to do something now, you have the potential to develop the necessary skills and abilities over time.

This simple change in language helps transition from a fixed mindset, where you believe your talents are static, to a growth mindset, where you see them as malleable and capable of development.

**Exercise**: Try this out in your own life. Practice adding "yet" to your daily conversations and thoughts. Notice how this change in language influences your mindset and approach to challenges. You might be surprised at the boost in your motivation and persistence.

## 2. Focus on the Process, Not Just the Outcome

Unlike a fixed mindset, a growth mindset encourages you to value the journey and the steps taken along the way rather than just the final destination. Focusing only on the outcome makes it easy to become discouraged if things don't go as planned. However, when you value the process, you recognize that each step and each mistake is a part of your growth. This mindset helps you stay motivated and resilient, even when slow progress or setbacks occur.

**Exercise**: Reflect on a recent project or goal you had. Write down the steps you took, the effort you put in, and the lessons you learned. Acknowledge the process, not just the outcome. This way, you'll find joy in the journey and stay motivated for the long haul.

## 3. Cultivate Curiosity and a Love of Learning

This mindset thrives on curiosity and a passion for learning new things. When you're curious, you're more likely to explore new ideas, seek new knowledge, and challenge yourself to grow. Curiosity drives you to ask questions, investigate, and improve your understanding of the world. This love of learning helps you stay engaged and motivated as it evokes a sense of wonder and excitement about the possibilities ahead.

**Exercise**: Pick a topic or skill you're curious about and dedicate weekly time to explore and learn about it. Think about how this curiosity enhances your growth mindset. You'll find that the more you learn, the more you want to learn.

## 4. Surround Yourself with Growth-Oriented People

The people you spend time with significantly influence your mindset and behavior. It's hard not to adopt the same mindset when you're around people who believe in growth and learning. Their attitudes and behaviors can be contagious, and the positive influence can help you stay motivated and focused on your personal growth.

**Exercise**: Take a look at the people in your network. Who are those with a growth mindset? Work on strengthening your relationships with them. At the same time, consider joining groups or communities that instill a growth mindset. Being in such an environment can be incredibly inspiring and motivating.

By now, it should be clearer how these strategies can profoundly change your mindset and approach to life. Implement them and see how they improve your approach to challenges, learning, and personal development.

Here's a more practical exercise to further help you on this growth journey:

## Step 1: Identify Fixed Mindset Triggers

We all have moments when our fixed mindset sneaks in and takes over. It's helpful to pinpoint those triggers. Understanding the "why" can help you tackle these thoughts head-on.

• Spend 10-15 minutes reflecting on recent experiences where you felt stuck or defeated.
• List at least three specific situations that triggered a fixed mindset. For example:
➢ "When I couldn't solve a math problem quickly."
➢ "When I received critical feedback at work."
➢ "When I struggled to learn a new skill in my hobby."

- Next to each situation, write down why you think it triggered a fixed mindset. Was it fear of failure, past experiences, or something else?

## Step 2: Reframe Negative Thoughts

Negative thoughts can be persistent, but you can train yourself to see things differently. You don't have to be perfect right away. It's about the journey of growth.

- For each fixed mindset trigger, write down the negative thoughts you had. For example:
➤ "I'm not smart enough to understand this."
- Rewrite each negative thought from a growth mindset perspective. For example:
➤ "I'm not smart enough to understand this" becomes "I can improve my understanding by studying and asking for help."
- Choose one or two reframed thoughts and turn them into daily affirmations. Repeat these affirmations each morning for a week.

## Step 3: Set Learning Goals

Instead of setting performance, try setting learning goals. What new skills do you want to develop? What knowledge do you want to gain? Concentrate on learning to take the pressure off and allow yourself to enjoy the process.

- Think about the areas where you want to grow. Write down at least three skills or areas of knowledge you want to develop. For example:
➤ "Improve my public speaking skills," "Learn basic coding," and "Understand financial planning."
- Set Specific, Measurable, Achievable, Relevant, and Time-bound (SMART) learning goals for each area. For example:
➤ "I will practice public speaking by joining a local Toastmasters club and giving at least one speech monthly."

- Create a weekly action plan for each goal. Break down the steps you must take each week to move closer to your goal.

Don't wait until you've reached the finish line to celebrate. Recognize the effort you're putting in right now. It's important to track your progress, no matter how small. Maybe you practiced a new language for ten minutes today or finally understood a tricky concept. These are wins!

### Summing It Up

Adopting a growth mindset is key to personal and professional growth. You unlock your potential when you take on challenges, learn from feedback, push through setbacks, and see effort as the way to mastery. Embrace a growth mindset now if you want to boost your abilities and achieve long-term success.

# Key Takeaways

- A growth mindset fosters resilience, a love of learning, and the ability to embrace challenges as opportunities for growth.
- Embracing the power of "yet," focusing on the process, cultivating curiosity, and surrounding yourself with growth-oriented people are key strategies for developing a growth mindset.
- Regular reflection and intentional practice can help you shift from a fixed mindset to a growth mindset.

### Looking Ahead

Congratulations! You've completed the Internal Revolution. This is a big deal and a huge step towards adopting the Life-Work Revolution. Take a moment to celebrate. Now, we move on to the External Revolution. In the next chapter, we'll explore adapting to Career 4.0 and navigating this modern work landscape. How do you stay relevant and competitive in a fast-changing world? These principles will guide you. Get ready to use your newfound internal strengths in the external world!

# Part 3:
## The External Revolution - Navigating the Modern Work Landscape

After the internal revolution comes the external revolution. As a professional, this phase isn't just about tweaking your resume or learning new software. There has to be a fundamental shift in how you approach your career, especially in this age of career 4.0.

I briefly explained an external revolution in an earlier chapter, but this time, we're diving deeper into the concept for the next three chapters.

The external revolution refers to the significant and ongoing changes happening in the external environment that affect our professional lives. These changes are driven by technological advancements, globalization, and shifting economic landscapes. Unlike an internal revolution, which focuses on personal growth and self-improvement, an external revolution emphasizes adapting to and leveraging these external changes to thrive professionally.

Staying static in your career is not an option. The external revolution is crucial because it:

- keeps you relevant
- facilitates personal development and growth
- increases your flexibility
- makes you more innovative

The external revolution is about embracing career 4.0, creating a skills inventory, and establishing a dynamic career strategy. If you can take all three steps successfully, you can stay ahead of the curve no matter what.

We will explore each step from chapters 7 to 9 to help you begin and achieve the external revolution.

Get ready to take your career to a whole new level when you implement the strategies of the external revolution!

# Chapter 7:
## Adapting to Career 4.0

Many believe career 4.0 is a mere buzzword, but it is much more than that. It is the next step in the evolution of our professional lives. You might be wondering, what exactly does this term mean? In simple terms, Career 4.0 refers to the way our careers are transforming in response to the fourth industrial revolution. This revolution is driven by technological advancements, especially artificial intelligence, robotics, the Internet of Things (IoT), and big data.

### TIMELINE VISUALIZATION

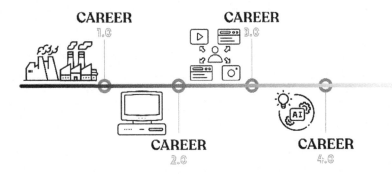

Think about how work has changed over the last few decades. We've gone from typewriters to computers, from landlines to smartphones. But the shift we're seeing now is even more profound. Career 4.0 is about adapting to a world where automation and AI are becoming commonplace. It's not just about new tools but new ways of thinking and working.

In this chapter, we will explore how you can adapt to these changes, develop strategies for staying relevant, and thrive in the dynamic environment of Career 4.0.

## The Evolution of Careers

To help you understand Career 4.0, we must take a quick look at the evolution of career models over the centuries.

### Career 1.0: Company as Career (1950s-1980s)

Working for a single company your entire career was the norm back in the day. Employees would often stick with one employer, sometimes even one job, until retirement. This era was about loyalty and tenure, where career growth was a slow but steady climb up the company ladder. Remember companies like IBM and GE? They were the gold standards of this model.

### Career 2.0: Your Work as Your Career (1980s-1990s)

Fast forward to the 1980s and 1990s, and things started to shift. Job networks and online job boards became game-changers. Now, employees take control of their own career paths, jumping from job to job to find the best growth opportunities. Companies like LinkedIn and Monster.com made finding new job openings easier than ever and connecting with potential employers. It was a time of exploration and rapid career movement.

### Career 3.0: You as Career (2000s-2020s)

Then came the gig economy and the rise of flexible work arrangements. Careers became much more adaptable. People could choose who they worked for, where they worked, and how they worked. Platforms like Uber, Upwork, and Coursera emerged, supporting this new working method. It was all about finding the perfect fit for your lifestyle and preferences.

### Career 4.0: Your Skills as Your Career (Today and Beyond)

Now, we're in the era of Career 4.0. This model is all about skills. Instead of focusing on job titles or long tenures, today's careers are defined by what you can do. Internal talent marketplaces and skills-based hiring are becoming the norm. Continuous learning and skill development are key. Employers are looking for versatile employees who can bring diverse skills and experiences to the table, often across different roles and industries. Modern companies across various sectors are emphasizing skills over traditional job titles.

What this shows is that careers have evolved from being company-centric to skill-centric. It's not about where you work or how long you stay; it's about what you bring to the table. In Career 4.0, your skills are your most valuable asset.

## Key Traits of Career 4.0

Career 4.0 has many key features that distinguish it from previous career models. Here are some of those traits:

**1. Skills as the New Currency**: In Career 4.0, skills drive career growth. Employers value your capabilities and potential more than job titles or tenure. Developing relevant and adaptable skills can significantly boost your career opportunities, making you a valuable asset in any industry.

**2. Dynamic Work Environment**: The rapid pace of technological change means that the skills needed today may differ from those required tomorrow. Staying informed about emerging trends ensures you remain competitive and adaptable.

**3. Technology as a Multiplier**: Emerging technologies like AI enhance productivity and outcomes. These tools allow you to accomplish more with less effort, turning you into a "super worker." Leveraging technology can significantly optimize your workflow.

**4. Internal Talent Marketplaces**: Organizations now offer internal platforms where employees can explore new roles, projects, and opportunities based on their skills and interests. This promotes internal mobility and continuous development.

**5. Continuous Learning and Development**: Gone are the days when you could learn a trade or profession and stick with it for life. In the Career 4.0 landscape, continuous learning is crucial. Upskilling and reskilling will be ongoing processes.

**6. Flexible Career Paths**: Career paths are no longer linear. Moving across different functions, industries, and roles driven by your skills and aspirations is now common. Thus, building a diverse skill set enhances your career flexibility and opportunities.

**7. Personalization and Autonomy**: You have greater control over your career trajectory. Choosing projects, roles, and learning opportunities that align with your personal and professional goals allows for a more fulfilling career path.

The above are some of the key traits of Career 4.0. Now, the question is how can you adapt and thrive in this modern work environment? Below, I'll share some strategies that have been incredibly life-changing for me.

## Strategies for Thriving in Career 4.0

Career 4.0 is all about adaptation and growth. It's a dynamic, ever-changing landscape that offers both challenges and opportunities. With the following strategies, you will not only adapt but thrive in this new era of work.

### 1. Embrace Lifelong Learning

Since continuous learning is key to staying relevant and competitive, it helps to learn new skills and expand one's knowledge base in career 4.0. That is how you stay ahead of the curve. Consider Sarah, who dedicates weekly time to online courses and professional development workshops. This ensures her skills remain current and valuable.

Have you thought about what new skills could boost your career? Maybe it's time to sign up for that course you've been eyeing or attend a local workshop.

## 2. Develop a Story Brand

Building a strong story brand is essential for enhancing your visibility and credibility in your industry. It's about showcasing your skills, values, and unique contributions. Take Reggie, for instance. He develops his story brand by sharing insights and expertise on social media and in industry publications, establishing himself as a thought leader.

How can you better share your expertise and insights to establish yourself as a thought leader? Perhaps you could start a blog, contribute articles to industry sites, or engage more on LinkedIn to share your unique perspective.

## 3. Cultivate Adaptability and Resilience

Embracing change and seeing challenges as opportunities for growth can make a big difference in career 4.0. Consider Brooks, who practices resilience by maintaining a positive outlook and seeking solutions during challenging times. This ensures he can bounce back and thrive.

How do you handle change, and what can you do to strengthen your resilience? Maybe mindfulness practices or stress management techniques could help enhance your adaptability.

## 4. Leverage Technology for Growth

Technology is a powerful tool that can enhance your productivity, creativity, and innovation. Integrating the right digital tools into your workflow can make you more efficient and effective. Emily, for example, uses digital tools to streamline her work processes and enhance her creative output, making her a more efficient and effective professional.

What new technologies could you explore to improve your performance? Whether it's project management software, creative design tools, or productivity apps, there's always something new to try that could make a significant impact.

Let me share my own story about how I implemented these strategies to navigate Career 4.0 and facilitate accelerated career growth.

**My Journey as a Future of Work Executive**

In my recent executive and advisory roles, I have helped organizations build talent marketplaces and redesign processes to become more skills-enabled. This shift allows data-driven insights on skills and capabilities to inform talent investment decisions on a large scale. It democratizes employee access to opportunities, making it easier for everyone to find the right fit.

By facilitating personalized experiences, we empower people to upskill and right-skill at their own pace. This flexibility boosts agility in getting work done and improves overall job satisfaction. Employees feel more engaged and motivated when they can see clear paths for their development.

Improving agility within organizations is crucial. When teams adapt quickly, they can respond better to changing business needs. This adaptability leads to better business results, as companies can stay ahead of the curve and handle challenges more effectively.

Helping companies become truly skills-enabled changes how work gets done and how people grow and thrive in their careers. As a thought leader, I advocate for these innovations to create a more dynamic and fulfilling work environment.

Here are some key aspects of my approach:

• **Continuous Learning**: I prioritize my own lifelong learning by staying updated on industry trends in HR, Learning Development,

Talent Development, AI, and emerging technologies. This has allowed me to pivot across different roles and industries successfully.

- **Building High-Value Networks**: I invest time building and nurturing professional relationships, providing invaluable support and collaboration opportunities.
- **Leveraging Technology**: I embrace technology to enhance productivity and innovation, ensuring I can achieve more with less effort and creating time for higher-order strategic work.
- **Developing My Story Brand**: My story brand reflects my expertise, values, and unique contributions to future work and skills development, allowing me to create leverage for new and interesting work opportunities and experiences.

## Exercise: Crafting Your Career 4.0 Strategy

This exercise will help you develop a comprehensive strategy for advancing your career in the modern work environment.

### 1. Identify Key Skills

*Action*: List your top five skills relevant to your job or industry.

*Example*: If you work in digital marketing, your skills might include SEO, content creation, data analysis, social media management, and email marketing. Identify which of these are rare and valuable. For instance, advanced data analysis might be rare but highly valuable in today's job market.

*Task*: Choose one of these key skills and plan to enhance it. For example, if advanced data analysis is your focus, enroll in a course on advanced analytics tools like Google Analytics 4 or Tableau.

### 2. Set Up Learning Sprints

*Action*: Develop a weekly learning plan.

*Example*: Allocate an hour every Friday to review the latest industry trends and technologies. Subscribe to relevant newsletters, such as MarketingProfs or Data Science Weekly. Use a learning platform like Coursera or Udemy to find courses that match your interests.

*Task*: Set a specific learning goal, such as completing a course on machine learning within the next two months.

### 3. Build and Curate Your Network

*Action*: Map your professional network by listing key contacts who can help with your career growth.

*Example*: Identify five people you want to connect with, such as a former colleague, a mentor, or an industry leader.

*Task*: Plan to reach out to one of these contacts each month. Send a personalized email or LinkedIn message, perhaps requesting a virtual coffee chat to discuss industry trends or seek advice on skill development.

### 4. Leverage Technology

*Action*: Identify technologies that can improve your workflow or productivity.

*Example*: If you manage multiple projects, consider using a project management tool like Asana or Trello. Explore advanced Excel functions or tools like Power BI if you frequently analyze data.

*Task*: Choose one technology to integrate into your workflow. For instance, if you select Trello, create a board for managing your daily tasks and set up automation rules to streamline your processes.

Follow these steps to create a clear, actionable career development plan leveraging your strengths and new growth opportunities.

### Summing It Up

Adapting to career 4.0 means embracing lifelong learning and crafting a compelling personal brand. It's about staying adaptable and resilient while using technology to your advantage. If you focus on the key strategies in this chapter, you can remain relevant, competitive, and successful in today's ever-changing work environment.

## Key Takeaways

- Rapid technological advancements and the need for continuous learning and adaptability characterize Career 4.0.
- Developing rare, valuable, and durable skills is essential for long-term career success.
- Building high-value networks and leveraging technology are critical strategies for thriving in Career 4.0.
- Embracing lifelong learning, cultivating adaptability, and developing a story brand are key components of a successful Career 4.0 strategy.
- Internal talent marketplaces and personalized career paths enable employees to explore diverse opportunities and continuously develop their skills.
- Skills-informed organizations can democratize access to opportunities and drive business results through talent agility and autonomy.

### Looking Ahead

The next chapter will focus on creating your skills inventory as we continue our journey through the External Revolution. This essential step will help you assess and develop your skill sets, ensuring you remain even more competitive and future-ready in the modern work landscape.

# Chapter 8:
## Creating Your Skills Inventory

Imagine you're about to start a new project, whether building a birdhouse or fixing a leaky faucet. You'd first check what tools you have and what you might need. A skills inventory works the same way. It lists your current abilities and knowledge and those you might need to develop. Just like checking your toolbox helps determine if you're ready for the job or need to pick up some extra tools, a skills inventory enables you to figure out where you stand in your career or personal growth.

## SKILL INVENTORY MAP
### RELEVANCE TO CAREER GOALS
**ADVANCED**

S
K
I
L
L

HIGH SKILL/LOW RELEVANCE | HIGH SKILL/HIGH RELEVANCE

**LOW**                  **HIGH**

L
E
V
E
L

LOW SKILL/LOW RELEVANCE | LOW SKILL/HIGH RELEVANCE

**BASIC**

This chapter will guide you through assessing your current skills, identifying areas for growth, and creating a roadmap for continuous development.

91

## Why You Need a Skills Inventory

Creating a skills inventory is a crucial part of the external revolution and is essential for dynamic career pathways in Career 4.0. As a comprehensive list of your abilities, knowledge, and experiences, a skills inventory helps you understand your strengths, identify gaps, and align your skills with your career aspirations and work-vision.

The World Economic Forum reports that the half-life of a learned skill is now about five years. This means that, on average, the skills you learn today will become half as valuable in just five years. To stay competitive and relevant in your career, it's crucial to update and expand your skill set continuously. This ensures that you remain proficient and adaptable.

Knowing your skills helps you understand your strengths. This knowledge alone can make career changes or promotions clearer. It translates job descriptions, aligns your abilities with job requirements, and targets your job search.

A skills inventory also boosts your networking. When you know your skills, you can communicate them confidently and leave a strong impression in interviews and networking events. If you haven't started one yet, now's the time. Your future career will thank you.

## Steps to Create Your Skills Inventory

Here's a step-by-step of how to create your skills inventory:

### 1. Identify Your Current Skills

Start by listing all your current skills. Include hard skills (technical abilities) and human-centered skills (soft skills). This will give you a clear picture of what you bring.

*Hard Skills*: Data analysis, programming, project management.

*Human-Centered Skills*: Communication, leadership, problem-solving.

To help identify your skills, you can refer to job descriptions, performance reviews, and colleague feedback.

## 2. Assess the Value of Your Skills

Next, evaluate the relevance and demand for each skill in your industry. Which skills are highly sought after? Which ones might become obsolete soon? Rate each skill on a scale from 1 to 5 based on its relevance and demand in your industry. According to McKinsey, the demand for technological, social, and emotional skills will rise by 2030, while the demand for basic cognitive skills will decline.

## 3. Identify Skills Gaps

Compare your current skills with the skills required for your desired career path. This will help identify any gaps in further development or new skills. Then, make a list of skills you need to develop. Prioritize them based on their importance to your career aspirations.

## 4. Create a Skills Development Strategy

Now, develop a strategy to acquire and enhance your skills. This strategy should include specific actions, resources, and timelines for achieving your skill development goals. For each skill you need to develop, you can list actions you can take (e.g., online courses, workshops, mentorship) and set a timeline for completion.

## 5. Create and Protect Time for Learning

You must regularly update your skills and knowledge to ensure lifelong learning. Identify learning resources relevant to your career aspirations. Create and protect a learning schedule and allocate weekly time for skill development. Experiment and apply knowledge to develop skills and evidence them.

## 6. Leverage Communities of Practice

Engaging with communities of practice can significantly boost your learning and skill development. By this, I mean groups of individuals who share a common interest and engage in collective learning. These communities are critical for skill development and knowledge sharing. According to Wenger-Trayner, communities of practice facilitate learning by providing opportunities for members to share experiences, solve problems collectively, and develop professionally.

Imagine being part of a group where everyone shares your passion and goals. Doesn't that sound motivating? Joining such a community allows you to gain insights from others, share your knowledge, and continuously improve your skills. The shared experiences and collective wisdom can help you grow faster and more efficiently than going it alone.

## 7. Incorporate Financial Discipline

As I explained, financial discipline is crucial for controlling your career and life decisions, especially in the modern economy. Developing good habits around earning, saving, and investing empowers you to make choices that align with your values. When you manage your finances well, you create the freedom to pursue opportunities that matter to you. This discipline helps you thrive beyond the typical 9-to-5 routine, giving you the flexibility to explore and achieve your goals.

## 8. Leverage High-Value Skills

Using your high-value skills for additional income can be a game-changer. Whether through freelance work, consulting, or learning new skills, you can create a valuable skill set that pays dividends over time. Identifying and marketing these skills allows you to earn more and build a reputation in your field. Maximizing your earnings without investing too much is easy if you focus on tasks with high outcome value and higher transaction prices. This strategic approach helps you fund other ventures and secure your financial future.

With these steps, you can create a comprehensive skills inventory that helps you stay competitive and achieve your career goals.

## Skills Inventory Exercise

Here's a practical, example-based exercise for creating a skills inventory:

### Step 1: Identify Current Skills

List your hard and human-centered skills.

- Hard Skills: _____
- Human-Centered Skills: _____

### Step 2: Assess Value

Rate the relevance and demand of each skill on a scale from 1 to 5 (1 being least relevant/in demand, 5 being most relevant/in demand). For example:

- *Project Management*: Relevance - 4, Demand - 5
- *Data Analysis*: Relevance - 5, Demand - 5
- *Programming (Python)*: Relevance - 4, Demand - 4
- *Graphic Design*: Relevance - 3, Demand - 3
- *Communication*: Relevance - 5, Demand - 5
- *Teamwork*: Relevance - 5, Demand - 4
- *Problem-Solving*: Relevance - 5, Demand - 5
- *Leadership*: Relevance - 4, Demand - 4
- Skill: _____, Relevance: __, Demand: __
- Skill: _____, Relevance: __, Demand: __

### Step 3: Identify Gaps

Determine which skills you need to develop based on your ratings and career goals. For example, you may need to establish Advanced Python programming, strategic leadership, digital marketing, etc.

- Need to Develop: _____

## Step 4: Create a Development Strategy

Outline actions and timelines for skill development.

*Example 1*: Advanced Python Programming

- Action: Enroll in an online course
- Timeline: Complete within 3 months

*Example 2*: Strategic Leadership

- Action: Attend leadership workshops
- Timeline: Participate in 2 workshops within 6 months

*Example 3*: Digital Marketing

- Action: Read industry books, follow experts on social media
- Timeline: Ongoing, with a focus on 1 book/month

*Example 4*: Skill: _____

- Action: _____
- Timeline: _____

## Step 5: Create and Protect Time for Learning

Allocate regular time for continuous learning. For example:

- Monday, Wednesday, Friday: 7-8 PM (Python Programming)
- Saturday: 10 AM-12 PM (Leadership Workshops)
- Sunday: 4-5 PM (Digital Marketing Reading)

*Weekly Learning Schedule*: _____

## Step 6: Incorporate Financial Discipline

Develop a financial plan to support your long-term goals. Leverage your high-value skills for additional income to build financial independence.

*Example*:

- Save 20% of income monthly
- Invest in a retirement fund
- Use programming skills for freelance projects to earn extra income

*Financial Plan*: _____

Feel free to tailor these steps to your specific needs and career goals.

### Summing It Up

By assessing your current skills, identifying gaps, engaging in continuous learning, and leveraging your high-value skills for additional income, you can stay competitive and future-ready in a rapidly evolving job market.

## Key Takeaways

- A skills inventory helps you understand your strengths and identify areas for growth.
- Evaluate the relevance and demand for your skills to focus on developing high-value, durable skills.
- Engage with communities of practice for support and collaboration.
- Commit to lifelong learning to keep your skills updated and relevant.
- Incorporate financial discipline to support your long-term goals and provide career flexibility.

### Looking Ahead

In the next chapter, we'll use your skills inventory to craft a dynamic career strategy. This strategy will guide you through Career 4.0, helping you leverage your skills to create fulfilling and successful career paths. We'll dive into practical steps and tactics to keep you adaptable, competitive, and ready to thrive in today's work environment. Ready to get started? Let's dive even deeper into the external revolution.

# Chapter 9:
## Building a Dynamic Career Strategy

In Career 4.0, it's time to rethink the traditional idea of a linear career path. Instead of just climbing the ladder, picture your career as a lattice. This means you can move sideways to where the work is, apply your skills to tackle business challenges and gain experiences that boost your credibility and relevance. This chapter will help you develop a dynamic career strategy. We'll focus on building skills, gaining experiences, experimenting, iterating, and finding opportunities that match your values and business goals.

## Reframing Career Paths

Think about the traditional career path for a moment. It usually means a straight line of progress within a specific job cluster, right? But today, that idea feels a bit outdated. Careers have become more dynamic, stretching across different roles, industries, and skill sets. Have you ever considered how this shift could benefit both employees and organizations?

According to a report by Deloitte, companies that encourage non-linear career paths often see a boost in employee engagement and retention. Why? Because when you, as an employee, see diverse career growth opportunities, you're more likely to stay with that organization. This means less turnover and more continuity, which can be crucial for long-term success. Plus, employees with experience in different business areas can bring fresh perspectives and innovative solutions.

So, what does this mean for you? Adopting a more flexible approach to career development keeps you engaged and opens up many possibilities you might not have considered before.

Picture working for a company that supports your growth in various directions. One day, you might deepen your expertise in your current field; the next, you might explore a new area that piques your interest. This kind of environment can be incredibly motivating.

Let's explore what a dynamic career strategy comprises.

## Key Components of a Dynamic Career Strategy

The following provides a structured approach to building relevant skills, navigating career transitions, and effectively advancing to higher-demand roles, making them the key components of a dynamic career strategy. They ensure you stay adaptable, competitive, and prepared for future opportunities.

### 1. Skills Adjacencies

Skills adjacencies help you transition smoothly between roles by leveraging related skills. They allow you to build on your existing capabilities while acquiring new ones. For example, when Sarah moved from a marketing role to a product management role, she used her customer insights and project management skills to make this transition successful.

*Exercise*: Identify related skills that can help you transition to new roles. Create a plan to develop these skills through courses, projects, or mentoring.

### 2. Development Steps

Career pathways include various development steps such as education, certifications, learning programs, experiences, and mentoring. Each step equips you with the skills needed for higher-demand roles. Take Reggie, for example. He takes on new projects, attends workshops, and seeks certifications to prepare for a leadership role in AI.

*Exercise*: Outline the development steps needed to reach your career goals. Include formal education, on-the-job experiences, and informal learning opportunities.

## 3. Understanding Roles: Feeder, Gateway, Destination, and High-Skill

Knowing the different types of roles can help you map out your career journey:

- Feeder Roles: Entry-level or declining roles that serve as starting points.
- Gateway Roles: Transition roles that help you develop skills for a different career in the long term.
- Destination Roles: Highly valued roles where you become a specialist.
- High-Skill Roles: Advanced roles that allow for continued career growth beyond destination roles.

For example, Emily starts in a feeder role as a data analyst, transitions through a gateway role in data science, and ultimately reaches a high-skill role in AI research.

*Exercise*: Research the common feeder, gateway, destination, and high-skill roles in your field. List the skills required for each type of role. Develop a step-by-step plan to move from one role to the next, then work on gaining the necessary skills and experiences.

## 4. Creating Leverage through Skills and Experiences

Building a diverse set of skills and experiences creates leverage, which opens you up to new opportunities. Consider Brooks, who leverages his project management and digital transformation skills to move across different industries.

*Exercise*: Identify opportunities to gain diverse experiences. Volunteer for cross-functional projects, create projects, or seek roles in different industries.

## 5. Understanding Skills Types

High-value skills are highly sought after in your desired industry or domain. On the flip side, low-value skills may be easily automated or delegated. The former can significantly impact your career growth and open up more opportunities for advancement, whereas the latter offers less impact. Understanding the difference in both types of skills can help you prioritize your efforts and focus on what truly matters.

Take Emily, for example. Her expertise in data analytics is highly valued in the tech industry, making her a sought-after professional. She didn't just stumble upon these skills; she identified them as crucial to her field and invested time in mastering them.

*Exercise*: Research the high-value skills in your target industry. Which ones can you start working on today to enhance your career prospects? Next, list the tasks you do regularly and identify low-value ones. Are there tools or software that can automate these tasks? Can you delegate them to free up your time for more strategic activities?

## 6. Applying and Contextualizing Learning

Taking courses and acquiring new knowledge is only one part of the learning equation. You need to apply and contextualize what you've learned to benefit truly. This closes the learning loop and ensures that new skills stick.

Once Sarah joined a marketing community of practice, she didn't just stop learning new strategies from them. Instead, she applied them in real scenarios and received valuable feedback from her peers.

*Exercise*: Identify communities of practice relevant to your field. These can be online forums, local meetups, or professional organizations. Join these communities, participate actively, and apply your new knowledge in real-world scenarios.

## 7. Creating Projects and Volunteering

If you can't find opportunities to apply your skills in your current role, creating projects or volunteering is the next best step. This approach is game-changing because it helps you gain practical experience and develop your capabilities, even outside your job. Look at Reggie. He couldn't find opportunities at work to use his AI skills, so he volunteered for a non-profit organization.

*Exercise*: Identify areas where you can create projects or volunteer. Think about causes you care about or areas where your skills can make a difference. Start contacting organizations or proposing projects that allow you to apply and develop your skills.

## 8. Guided Mentorship and Coaching

Guided mentorship and coaching accelerate skill development and behavior change through personalized support and accountability. A good mentor or coach can offer insights you might not gain alone. Take Emily again. She sought mentorship from a senior leader in her field. This relationship helped her develop her leadership skills, significantly boosting her professional growth.

According to a study by the International Journal of Evidence-Based Coaching and Mentoring, mentorship significantly enhances career satisfaction, skill development, and professional growth. This underscores the value of finding a good mentor or coach as part of your career strategy.

*Exercise*: Seek out mentors or coaches who can provide guidance and support. Look within your organization, professional networks, or online platforms. Engage in regular mentoring sessions and actively apply the feedback and advice you receive. Who can you reach out to today for mentorship?

103

I created a dynamic career strategy by understanding and taking advantage of these components, and you can, too. Doing so will ensure you're adaptable and ready for the next opportunity.

**My Journey as a Consultant to Thought Leader**

My tenure at Accenture and developing a strategic growth mindset and high-value transferable skill sets helped me navigate career pathways across functions and industries based on my life-work design and intentions. I learned to think of career paths not as ladders but as lattices, where the key is to move to where the work is, apply my skills to solve business challenges and gain experiences that enhance my credibility and relevance. Here are some key aspects of my approach:

- **Comprehensive Skill Assessment**: I regularly assess my durable skills and identify areas for improvement. This helps me stay ahead of industry trends and continuously develop my capabilities.
- **Intentions and Planning**: I set clear intentions for skill growth and create detailed design intentions to achieve them. This approach ensures continuous growth and alignment with my work aspirations.
- **Leveraging Opportunities**: I use my skills inventory to identify and pursue work opportunities that align with my strengths and interests. This strategy has enabled me to take on diverse and fulfilling roles and to experiment with low risk.
- **Continuous Learning**: I prioritize lifelong learning by engaging in masterminds, communities, courses, workshops, and professional development programs. This commitment ensures my skills remain relevant and valuable. I also teach, volunteer, and advise regularly as a learning technique.

## Exercise for Building a Dynamic Career Strategy

In this exercise, I will walk you through practical steps to build a dynamic career strategy for yourself. Let's get started.

**Step 1: Document Experiences**

*Objective: Record your professional experiences, projects, and achievements.*

**Activity**:

- Spend 30 minutes jotting down your key experiences from the past year. Focus on projects where you demonstrated significant skills.
- Use a template to structure your notes:
  - **Project Name:**
  - **Role:**
  - **Skills Demonstrated:**
  - **Achievements:**
  - **Outcome:**

*Example*:

- ***Project Name***: Website Redesign
- ***Role***: Project Manager
- ***Skills Demonstrated***: Leadership, Communication, Time Management
- ***Achievements***: Delivered the project two weeks ahead of schedule
- ***Outcome***: Increased user engagement by 20%

**Step 2: Set Development Goals**

*Objective: Set intentions for developing the skills identified in your inventory.*

**Activity**:

- Identify three key skills you want to improve. Write them down.
- For each skill, create a SMART goal (Specific, Measurable, Achievable, Relevant, Time-bound).
- Outline a timeline and action plan to achieve these goals.

*Example*:

- *Skill*: Public Speaking
- *Goal*: Deliver at least three presentations to different teams within the next six months.
- *Action Plan*: Enroll in a public speaking course, practice weekly, and seek peer feedback.

**Step 3: Align Skills with Opportunities**

*Objective: Use your skills inventory to identify career opportunities that match your strengths and interests.*

**Activity**:

- List your top five skills and interests.
- Research job roles or projects within your organization or industry that align with these skills.
- Note down at least three potential opportunities.

*Example*:

- *Skills*: Data Analysis, Problem-Solving, Project Management
- *Interests*: Tech Industry, Innovation, Team Collaboration
- *Opportunities*: Data Analyst role in a tech startup, Project Manager for an innovation project, Team Lead for a cross-functional project.

**Step 4: Communicate Your Value**

*Objective: Use your skills inventory to update your resume, LinkedIn profile, and professional portfolio.*

**Activity:**

- Revise your resume to highlight key skills and achievements.
- Update your LinkedIn profile summary to reflect your strengths and career goals.
- Add recent projects and skills to your professional portfolio.

*Example*:

- **Resume**: Under "Experience," ensure each role has bullet points showcasing skills and achievements.
- **LinkedIn**: Craft a summary of your career story, emphasizing your unique skills and goals.
- **Portfolio**: Include detailed case studies of significant projects.

## Step 5: Plan Career Development

**Objective**: *Develop a career development plan based on your skills inventory.*

**Activity**:

- Draft a career development plan outlining your short-term and long-term goals.
- Identify resources and opportunities for growth, such as courses, workshops, or networking events.

**Example**:

- **Short-term Goal**: Gain certification in Data Science within the next year.
- **Long-term Goal**: Transition to a Senior Data Analyst role in the next three years.
- **Resources**: Online courses, industry conferences, mentorship.

## Step 6: Leverage Talent Marketplaces

**Objective**: *Engage with your organization's internal talent marketplace.*

**Activity:**

- Explore your organization's internal talent marketplace.
- Use your skills inventory to identify and apply for relevant opportunities.

**Example:**

- *Marketplace Opportunities*: Project Lead for an upcoming data migration project, Training Coordinator for new software implementation.

## Step 7: Engage in Communities of Practice

*Objective: Actively participate in relevant communities of practice to apply and contextualize your learning.*

### Activity:

- Join at least one community of practice related to your field.
- Participate in discussions, share your experiences, and learn from others.

### *Example:*

- *Community*: Data Science Group on LinkedIn
- *Engagement*: Post weekly insights, ask questions, and contribute to discussions.

## Step 8: Seek Mentorship and Coaching

*Objective: Find mentors or coaches to guide you and provide accountability in your career development.*

### Activity:

- Identify potential mentors or coaches within your network.
- Reach out to them, explaining your career goals and asking for guidance.

### *Example:*

- Mentor: Senior Data Scientist in your organization
- Approach: Send an email or message on LinkedIn expressing your interest in mentorship and outlining your career aspirations.

You can tweak the steps in this practical exercise to build a dynamic career strategy specific to your goals, skills, and industry. Good luck!

**Summing It Up**

Creating and using a dynamic career strategy is essential for thriving in today's constantly evolving job market. These tips will enable you to stay ahead and prepare for the future. Most importantly, they will ensure you remain competitive and adaptable in the modern work environment.

# Key Takeaways:

- Career paths in Career 4.0 are more dynamic, focusing on leveraging skills and experiences to navigate opportunities rather than following a linear progression.
- Developing a comprehensive skills inventory helps you assess your current abilities, identify gaps, and set development goals.
- Understanding the difference between durable, perishable, high-value, and low-value skills allows for a strategic approach to skill development.
- Engaging in communities of practice and guided mentorship provides support and accelerates skill development and behavior change.
- Leveraging internal talent marketplaces and actively seeking diverse experiences enhances career growth and adaptability.

**Looking Ahead**

Congratulations on laying the groundwork for the External Revolution and getting a grip on Career 4.0! As we move forward, we're diving into an exciting new phase: the power of community. This next phase will show you how to build and harness networks that fuel your personal and professional growth. You will learn how to stay connected and supported in today's dynamic work environment. First, I have two bonus chapters for you on building your personal story brand and establishing yourself as a thought leader. So, let's get into that!

# Bonus Chapter I:
## External Revolution: Developing Your Story Brand

*"Your brand is what people say about you when you're not in the room."* – Jeff Bezos

Have you ever thought about the power of your personal story in shaping your career and facilitating financial independence? In today's world of Career 4.0, your story isn't just a narrative; it's a crucial asset. Your experiences, challenges, and triumphs make you unique and memorable.

This chapter will walk you through why your story brand matters, how to develop and nurture it, and ways to leverage it for continuous growth, success, and financial independence in your career.

### The Importance of a Story Brand

Your story brand is more than just a professional identity; it represents your values, skills, and unique contributions to your industry and community. It's not just about your skills or achievements; it's about who you are and what you stand for.

Think about it: what do you remember most when you meet someone new? Often, it's the stories they share. Your story brand can differentiate you from others, making you a 1:1 in your field and allowing you to stand out in a crowded market.

According to a study by CareerBuilder, 70% of employers use social media to screen candidates during the hiring process, and 50% of employers check current employees' social media profiles. This highlights the importance of maintaining a strong and positive personal brand online(career-pathways-research...).

Your story is a tool that can help you leverage capital. It speaks for you and goes with you no matter where you work or how many life-work revolutions you have. When you fuel your story with capital from your works, experiences, skills, and knowledge, it creates differentiation that becomes a key lever towards becoming a revolutionary and achieving both financial freedom and autonomy in life and work according to your values and views.

I'll share more on how to achieve financial independence and freedom in a subsequent chapter. For now, let's focus on building your brand.

## Building Your Story Brand

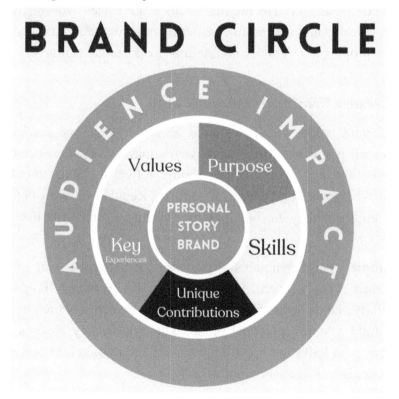

**BRAND CIRCLE**

Building a strong personal brand is all about strategically showcasing your skills, values, and unique qualities. It's like creating a narrative that highlights what makes you stand out. Here are some steps to help you develop a compelling personal story:

- **Identify Your Unique Value Proposition**

First, reflect on your skills, experiences, and values. What sets you apart from others in your industry? Think about how you can add value in ways that others might not. This process involves identifying what makes you unique and understanding how to leverage that in your career.

**Example**: Reggie is an international marketing executive who excels in cross-cultural communication and strategic market expansion. Through these, he has positioned himself uniquely in the marketing industry. He highlights his experiences working with diverse teams and successfully entering new markets as his unique value proposition. This is compelling to potential employers and clients.

- **Create a Consistent Online Presence**

Next, your online presence should be professional and consistent across all platforms. This means your LinkedIn, Twitter, personal website and any other profiles should reflect the same message about who you are and what you stand for. Regularly sharing content that aligns with your brand helps reinforce your expertise and values.

**Example**: Sarah maintains a professional and consistent online presence across LinkedIn, Twitter, and her personal blog. She regularly shares insights on leadership and diversity, which helped her build a strong personal brand. This consistency ensures that anyone who looks her up will get a clear and unified impression of who she is and what she stands for.

- **Network Authentically**

Networking isn't just about collecting business cards or making connections on LinkedIn. It goes beyond superficial interactions and extends to building genuine relationships. This is crucial for your personal brand. Engage authentically by attending industry events, participating in webinars, and joining online discussions. Being authentic and genuine can lead to more meaningful and lasting professional relationships.

**Example**: Brooks builds authentic relationships within his industry by attending conferences, participating in webinars, and engaging with peers on social media. For instance, after meeting someone at a conference, he would follow up with a personalized message, discussing shared interests or insights from the event. His genuine approach to networking strengthened his personal brand and has helped him form valuable connections based on mutual respect and shared interests.

- **Showcase Your Expertise**

Look for opportunities to showcase your expertise. This could be through speaking engagements, writing articles, or creating content highlighting your skills and experiences. Sharing your knowledge builds credibility and positions you as a thought leader in your field.

**Example**: Emily showcases her expertise by speaking at industry conferences, publishing articles, and sharing case studies of her work. For instance, she wrote a comprehensive article on successful project management strategies, drawing from her own experiences. This proactive approach has positioned her as a thought leader in her field, making her a go-to person for insights and advice in her industry.

Keep in mind that building a personal brand is an ongoing process. Ensure your messaging is uniform across all platforms and interactions. More importantly, stay true to your values and be authentic. Authenticity is key to maintaining credibility and building trust.

Once you've built a personal story brand, it's time to leverage it for opportunities. This step can provide significant career advantages.

## Leveraging Your Story Brand

Establishing your story brand is just the first step. The magic happens when you leverage it to unlock career opportunities and personal growth. When I say "leverage your personal brand," I mean using it to stand out and attract immense opportunities you otherwise wouldn't be privy to within and outside your field.

Here's how you can maximize the benefits of your personal story:

- **Use Your Story to Access Opportunities**

Your personal story is a powerful tool that can open doors to new opportunities. Identify areas where your story aligns with your career goals and interests. Don't hesitate to reach out to potential collaborators, apply for roles, and seek opportunities that resonate with your narrative.

**Example**: Sarah uses her personal story of overcoming adversity in her industry to secure speaking engagements at major conferences like TEDx and industry-specific events like the Women in Tech Summit.

- **Build Extensions of Your Story**

Expanding your personal story can help you reach a broader audience and establish yourself as a versatile expert. Think about launching a blog, starting a podcast, or creating a new initiative that aligns with your values and expertise. These platforms allow you to share more of your journey and connect with others who share your interests.

**Example**: I expanded my personal story by creating the Life-Work Revolution, a movement that supports life-work transformations through coaching, mentorship, digital content, and curated development experiences. This initiative broadened my reach and reinforced my brand as a leader in life-work balance and personal development.

- **Continuously Evolve Your Story**

Your personal story should evolve as you grow professionally and personally. Regularly review and update your story to reflect your skills, experiences, and aspirations. This ensures that your story remains relevant and aligns with your career growth.

**Example**: Reggie recently updated his personal story to showcase his latest AI and machine learning skills. He documented his journey from mastering basic programming languages to working on cutting-edge AI projects. He also highlighted his contributions to open-source projects and his role in mentoring junior developers. This proactive approach has kept his story fresh and relevant and increased his appeal.

Remember, an engaging story brand isn't just about telling your story. It's also about connecting with your audience. So, share your story in a way that resonates with them. Use social media, public speaking, and networking events to communicate your journey and values.

These tips allow you to leverage your personal brand to drive your career forward.

## My Core Story Brand Descriptors

- Father: Emphasizes the importance of family and work-life balance.
- **Investor**: Highlights strategic thinking and financial acumen.

- **Thought Leader**: Shares insights and innovations in the future of work.
- **Corporate Executive**: Demonstrates leadership and industry expertise.
- **Speaker**: Engages audiences with motivational and insightful presentations.
- **Coach**: Guides others through personal and professional growth.
- **Advocate**: Supports diversity, equity, and inclusion initiatives.
- **Entrepreneur**: Showcases innovation and business acumen.
- **Motivator**: Inspires others to reach their potential.
- **Athlete**: Promotes health, discipline, and perseverance.
- **Author**: Shares knowledge and experiences through writing.

Strategically developing and nurturing my personal story has enabled me to navigate networks, access opportunities, and continually grow professionally.

## Exercise: Developing Your Story

This exercise will show you how to identify your roles, define your unique value, create a story roadmap, and regularly reflect on and adjust your narrative. Ready to get started?

### Step 1: Identify Your Roles

List the different roles you play in your professional and personal life.

*Example:*

- Professional: Project Manager, Team Leader, Content Creator
- Personal: Parent, Mentor, Volunteer

*Actions:*

1. Take a piece of paper or open a document.
2. Write down every role you identify with at work and in your personal life.

3. Be comprehensive. Each role contributes to your overall story.

**Step 2: Define Your Value Proposition**

Clearly articulate what makes you unique and how you add value in each role.

*Example:*

- Project Manager: "I streamline project workflows to ensure timely delivery and high-quality outcomes."
- Mentor: "I foster a nurturing and supportive environment that encourages growth and curiosity."

*Actions:*

1. Write a brief statement highlighting your unique value for each role listed.
2. Focus on what you bring to the table that others might not.
3. Keep it straightforward.

**Step 3: Create a Story Roadmap**

Develop a roadmap for building and leveraging your personal story. Include strategies for online presence, networking, and showcasing your expertise.

*Example:*

- Online Presence: "Update LinkedIn profile to reflect new skills and projects."
- Networking: "Attend industry conferences and engage in relevant online forums."
- Showcasing Expertise: "Write and publish monthly blog posts on industry trends."

*Actions:*

1. Break down your story-building into actionable steps.
2. Decide on the platforms and methods you'll use to share your story.

3. Set realistic timelines for each action.

**Step 4: Reflect and Iterate**

Review your personal story and adjust as needed to align with your goals and industry trends.

*Example:*

- Monthly Review: "Check LinkedIn analytics to see which posts resonate most."
- Adjustments: "Based on feedback, focus on emerging trends in your field."

*Actions:*

1. Schedule regular check-ins (monthly or quarterly) to review your story.
2. Analyze what's working and what isn't.
3. Be flexible and ready to tweak your story to better align with your evolving goals and the latest industry trends.

**Summary**

- **Identify Your Roles**: List your professional and personal roles.
- **Define Your Value Proposition**: Articulate your unique value in each role.
- **Create a Story Roadmap**: Develop a strategy for building and sharing your story.
- **Reflect and Iterate**: Regularly review and adjust your personal story.

These practical tips will help you create a dynamic, authentic story brand that truly reflects who you are and what you stand for.

**Summing It Up**

Developing and leveraging your personal story is key to career growth and success. When you strategically build and nurture your story, you stand out in the market, unlock new opportunities, and grow professionally.

## Key Takeaways

- Your personal story is a powerful asset that represents your values, skills, and unique contributions.
- Building a personal story involves identifying your unique value proposition, creating a consistent online presence, networking authentically, and showcasing your expertise.
- Leveraging your personal story can open doors to new opportunities and help you build extensions of your story.
- Regularly review and update your personal story to keep it relevant and aligned with your career goals.

**Looking Ahead** As we conclude our exploration of developing your Story Brand, it's time to continue our journey through the External Revolution. The next chapter will focus on building influence and becoming a thought leader in your industry.

# Bonus Chapter II:
## External Revolution: Building Influence and Becoming a Thought Leader

In the words of Simon Sinek, "Leadership isn't about being in charge; it's about taking care of those in your charge." As you find your way around the world of Career 4.0, establishing yourself as a thought leader can significantly enhance your professional influence and open up new opportunities. But what does it mean to be a thought leader? It's about sharing your expertise, insights, and perspectives to inspire and guide others in your industry. Sounds impactful, right? This chapter will guide you through the steps to build your influence, develop thought leadership, and leverage it for career growth.

We'll begin by taking a closer look at thought leadership.

## Understanding Thought Leadership

Thought leadership is about positioning yourself as an authority in your field by sharing valuable insights and innovative ideas. It's not just about knowing but also about how you share it. Are you contributing to industry conversations? Are you providing solutions to common challenges? Are you inspiring others to think differently? That's the essence of thought leadership.

Research supports the importance of thought leadership in business. According to a study by Edelman and LinkedIn, 58% of decision-makers said thought leadership directly led them to award business to an organization. Even more compelling, 61% were more willing to pay a premium to work with a company that clearly articulates a vision through thought leadership.

So, what does this mean for you? It means that by sharing your expertise and unique perspectives, you can establish yourself as a leader in your industry and attract new business and opportunities. Thought leadership isn't just about being seen; it's about being heard and making a real impact. That way, you can become one of those driving change in your field.

## THOUGHT LEADER DIFFERENTIATION

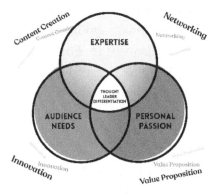

## Steps to Build Influence and Become a Thought Leader

Thought leadership is built on originality. To become a thought leader, you must consistently provide your audience with information that isn't already out there. They must know that you have the answers, opinions, research, and strategies –everything they need. Otherwise, they will go to someone else. That's how to build influence for your brand.

Here's what it takes to become a leader:

### 1. Choose a Niche

Your expertise will determine your niche. The objective is to become a thought leader in a field that you're exceptionally knowledgeable in. Naturally, you must consider your skills, interests, and experiences. Where do you have the most knowledge? Pinpointing a niche where you can offer unique insights and add value lays the foundation for your thought leadership journey. For instance, if you have extensive experience in digital marketing, you might focus on content strategy or social media trends.

## 2. Create and Share Valuable Content

Once you've identified your niche, start creating and sharing valuable content. This could be a blog, articles, videos, or podcasts. Consistently produce content that addresses key issues, trends, or challenges in your niche. Share your content on social media, industry platforms, and your website. For example, if your niche is content strategy, write about the latest SEO techniques, create video tutorials on keyword research, or start a podcast discussing successful content marketing campaigns.

## 3. Engage with Your Audience

Engagement is crucial for building influence. Respond to comments on your posts, participate in industry discussions, and host webinars or Q&A sessions. This interaction shows your audience that you value their input and are willing to engage with them on a deeper level. If your focus is social media trends, consider hosting live Q&A sessions on Instagram or Twitter to discuss recent platform updates and how businesses can adapt.

## 4. Speak at Industry Events

Seek out opportunities to speak at conferences, webinars, and industry events. Sharing your insights and experiences at these events can significantly boost your credibility and visibility. If you specialize in leadership development, look for conferences focusing on business management and offering to share your knowledge on building effective teams or navigating organizational change.

### 5. Network with other Thought Leaders

Connecting with other thought leaders in your industry can be incredibly beneficial. Attend events, join professional groups, and engage with other leaders online. Building these relationships can help you expand your influence, stay updated on industry trends, and open up new opportunities. If your niche is technology innovation, join tech forums, attend meetups, and participate in online discussions to connect with other innovators and thought leaders.

You'll need consistency and genuineness to establish and maintain your status as a thought leader. So, keep that in mind as you gradually build your influence.

## Leveraging Thought Leadership for Career Growth

Once you have established yourself as a thought leader, leveraging this influence can provide significant career advantages. Here are strategies to maximize the benefits of your thought leadership:

1. **Enhance Your Professional Reputation**: Use your thought leadership to build a strong professional reputation. Share your successes and showcase your expertise. For instance, if you've led a successful project, write about it on LinkedIn or your blog. Highlight your contributions to your industry by publishing case studies or whitepapers. This reinforces your credibility and keeps your audience engaged with your work.

2. **Attract New Opportunities**: Actively seek new opportunities aligning with your thought leadership. Reach out to potential collaborators, apply for roles that match your expertise, and explore new avenues for growth. For example, if you've become known for your innovative approach to digital marketing, consider applying for a speaking slot at an industry conference.

3. **Expand Your Network**: Another key strategy is to use your thought leadership to expand your network. Attend industry events, participate in online discussions, and connect with other professionals in your field. Join relevant LinkedIn groups or Twitter chats to share your insights and learn from others. Building a robust network can lead to new partnerships, mentorship opportunities, and increased visibility in your industry.

4. **Influence Industry Trends**: Finally, leverage your influence to shape industry trends and conversations. Share your insights on emerging topics, propose new ideas, and contribute to industry publications. For instance, if you notice a gap in current industry practices, write an article suggesting a new approach. Your unique perspective can drive meaningful change.

### My Personal Journey as a Thought Leader

I've built my personal brand and established myself as a thought leader by sharing my insights and experiences. Here's a glimpse into what defines my journey:

- **The Life-Work Revolution**: Through coaching, mentorship, digital content, and curated development experiences, I support professionals in their life-work transformations.
- **Father and Investor**: I balance professional success with personal fulfillment, emphasizing family and strategic thinking.
- **Corporate Executive and Speaker**: I speak at industry events about the future of work, leadership, and industry trends.
- **Coach and Advocate**: I guide others through personal and professional growth, championing diversity, equity, and inclusion.
- **Entrepreneur and Motivator**: I inspire innovation and business acumen, helping others reach their potential.
- **Athlete and Author**: I promote health, discipline, and perseverance, sharing my knowledge through writing.

I have leveraged my thought leadership successfully to expand my network, access opportunities, and grow professionally.

**Summing It Up**

Becoming a thought leader is key to boosting your professional influence and unlocking new opportunities. By strategically building and showcasing your expertise, you can stand out in the market, access new opportunities, and keep growing in your career.

# Key Takeaways

- Thought leadership involves sharing your expertise and insights to inspire and guide others.
- Building thought leadership includes identifying your niche, creating valuable content, engaging with your audience, speaking at events, and networking with other thought leaders.
- Leveraging thought leadership can enhance your professional reputation, attract new opportunities, expand your network, and influence industry trends.

Get ready to explore the Community Revolution! We'll explore how solid and supportive networks can boost your path to achieving a life-work balance and making a meaningful impact. It's time to connect, collaborate, and continue building towards your goals.

# Part 4:
## The Community Revolution - Building Supportive Networks and a Legacy Foundation

Welcome to Part 4 of the Life-Work Revolution: The Community Revolution. Humans need community. The community revolution refers to the significant shift in how we connect, interact, and collaborate within communities due to technological advancements and changes in social dynamics.

This revolution aims to reimagine how you support, engage, inspire, and uplift others – and vice versa. Embracing the community revolution can make a remarkable difference for you as a professional aiming to balance life and work. But what does this mean for you?

First, the community revolution is about building and leveraging networks of people who share common goals and interests. It means shifting from isolated work environments to collaborative, supportive communities. Imagine having a network of peers, mentors, and collaborators who help you grow and succeed. Sounds great, right?

Some benefits of the community revolution include:

• **Enhanced Collaboration**: Engaging in the community revolution allows you to collaborate more effectively. You'll have access to diverse perspectives and expertise, which can spark creativity and innovation in your work.

- **Networking Opportunities**: Participating in communities expands your network. This can open doors to new opportunities, partnerships, and career advancements you might not find alone.
- **Support Systems**: Communities provide a support system. Whether facing professional challenges or personal struggles, having a community means you're not alone. You have a safety net of people who can offer advice, support, and encouragement.
- **Flexibility and Balance**: The life-work revolution centralizes flexibility. Communities often support and encourage this, offering resources and spaces that help you manage your time better, reducing stress and burnout.
- **Personal Growth**: Being part of a community means continuous learning and growth. You'll be exposed to new ideas, skills, and knowledge, which can enhance both your personal and professional life.

In essence, embracing the community revolution as part of the overarching Life-Work Revolution means you can thrive in a more connected, supportive, and balanced environment. It's about working smarter, not harder, and finding joy in your professional achievements and personal pursuits.

In Chapter 10, we will look in-depth at the power of community.

# Chapter 10:
## The Power of Community

Building and leveraging a strong community is vital for personal and professional growth. Communities provide support, resources, and opportunities that can significantly enhance your journey. This chapter explores the importance of community in life and work, strategies for building high-value networks, and the role of mentorship and peer support in achieving your goals.

## The Power of Community

Communities play a vital role in our growth, providing support, accountability, and opportunities for learning and collaboration. Engaging with like-minded individuals and groups can significantly enhance your journey toward life-work synergy.

Throughout nearly two decades of working on people improvement in various organizations, I learned invaluable lessons about the value of community in different contexts. Communities have been instrumental in my growth, providing support, accountability, and opportunities for learning and collaboration. For example, I found immense value in joining professional groups and networks to share knowledge and learn from others.

### Communities for Growth and Development

Learning with others is one of the best ways to turn learning into skills and skills into experiences. It creates accountability, support, and a safe space for experimentation. For example, joining a mastermind group or a professional association can provide the resources and feedback necessary to grow. These communities offer diverse perspectives and collective wisdom, accelerating learning and development.

**Exercise**: Identify a professional association or mastermind group in your field. Commit to attending their meetings and actively participating in discussions.

**Communities for Building Networks**

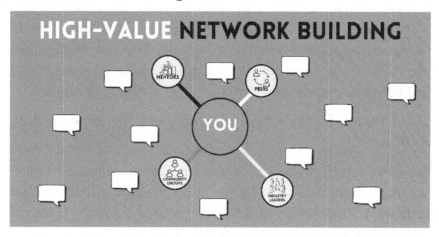

Building high-value networks through the lens of community is super helpful as you navigate growth and development. Hobbies, sports clubs, church, and classes are all venues where you can build meaningful connections. These networks provide not only professional opportunities but also personal fulfillment and support.

Participating in local community events or volunteering can help you meet people with similar interests and values. These connections can lead to unexpected opportunities and collaborations.

**Exercise**: Volunteer for a local event or join a community group related to your interests. Engage with members and look for opportunities to collaborate.

**Community for Giving Back and Building a Legacy**

We inspire others through our stories, kindness, and work. Recognizing your gifts and sharing them with others is the ultimate giveback. Writing this book is a form of giving back, along with my mission of providing marginalized groups with future-ready skills and opportunities. This drive to give back and build a legacy is a key aspect of the Life-Work Revolution.

It is part of why my wife and I started a family business and non-profit named after our fathers, grandfathers, and namesakes to impact others through affordable housing, financial literacy, and life-skills education. Something our daughters can be proud of and build on to help positively impact the lives and work of others.

### Case Study: Ghana's Independence and the Role of Seth Anthony

In Ghana, community and collaboration were vital during the post-colonial transition. The collective effort to achieve independence underscored the power of unity and shared purpose. Fostering relationships that support our growth and aspirations can mirror this community revolution in our lives.

Seth Anthony, my wife's belated grandfather, played a significant role in Ghana's journey to independence. His bravery and resilience inspired his family and community, instilling values passed down through generations. This story holds personal significance as I raise a half-Ghanaian family, and we strive to honor his legacy through our work.

- **Internal Revolution - The Will to Fight**: Seth Anthony's bravery and resilience were catalysts for the rise of Ghanaian nationalism. As a black officer in the British army during World War II, he faced immense racism and adversity. Despite these challenges, Anthony's unwavering determination and self-discipline allowed him to rise through the ranks, earning respect and recognition. His internal revolution fueled his ability to inspire

130

others and catalyze change, laying the groundwork for Ghana's independence.

- **External Revolution - The Fight for Freedom**: Ghana's road to achieving freedom and independence was marked by significant economic and social shifts. Independence meant controlling their financial destiny, reducing reliance on colonial powers, and fostering local entrepreneurship and education. For instance, the construction of the Akosombo Dam was a significant post-independence project aimed at boosting the economy and reducing dependency on foreign aid.

- **Community Revolution - Influence at Scale**: The shifts in Ghana's historical independence had far-reaching impacts, including influencing the US civil rights movement and other global liberation movements. The sense of community and collective effort in Ghana's struggle for independence underscored the power of unity and shared purpose, inspiring other marginalized communities to fight for their rights.

Seth Anthony's story shows us how community and collaboration can transform lives and societies. His bravery and resilience remind me of the powerful impact one person can have when driven by purpose and unity. It resonates deeply as I raise my half-Ghanaian family, honoring his legacy through our own commitments to growth and community.

Just as the fight for freedom sparked movements worldwide, you too can ignite change within your life and communities. To do this, though, you must first build your community.

## Building Your Community Network

Yes, it is absolutely possible to build your own community network. Whether you aim to connect a neighborhood, a group of friends, or a niche interest group, creating a community network is a great way to facilitate communication and collaboration. Here's how to do this:

- **Identify Your Communities**: List your current communities and consider potential new ones. Which of these resonate with your values and support your personal or professional goals?
- **Engage Actively**: Participation is key to getting the most out of any community. Set specific goals for your involvement, like attending a monthly meeting, participating in online forums, or volunteering for community projects.
- **Provide Value**: Communities thrive when members actively contribute. Think about your skills and knowledge and how you can use them to support others. Whether sharing expertise, offering support, or helping others achieve their goals, your contributions can make a big difference. Try to add value to each community you're part of.
- **Seek Support**: Building strong relationships is a two-way street. Don't hesitate to seek support from your community. Asking for help not only benefits you but also strengthens your connections. Reach out to community members when you need assistance, and be open to offering help when others seek it.
- **Foster Collaboration**: Encouraging collaboration within your community can lead to outstanding achievements. Work together on projects, share resources, and celebrate successes. By initiating collaborative projects and sharing resources, you can evoke a sense of unity and collective accomplishment.

These tips will help enhance your community involvement, leading to personal growth.

## Practical Exercise for Building Your Community Network

Here's a simple exercise to help you get started on building your community network:

## 1. List Your Goals

Think about what you want to achieve with your network. Are you looking for mentorship, job opportunities, or industry insights? Clearly define your goals. This will guide your networking efforts and help you connect with the right people.

## 2. Create a List of Key Contacts

Write down people you already know who can support your career goals. Include colleagues, former classmates, and industry professionals. Next, list individuals you want to meet, like thought leaders or potential mentors in your field.

## 3. Plan Outreach Strategies

Decide how you'll reach out to these contacts. Will you use LinkedIn messages, email introductions, or attend industry events? For instance, if you're interested in marketing, you might join a marketing association and attend their events.

## 4. Craft Personalized Messages

When reaching out, personalize your communication. Mention any mutual connections or specific reasons for your interest. For example, if you're contacting a potential mentor, briefly explain why you admire their work and how they can help you.

## 5. Follow Up and Engage

Once you make initial contact, follow up to maintain the relationship. Share relevant articles, congratulate them on their achievements, or ask for a brief coffee chat. Keep the interaction genuine and mutual.

Make sure to track your networking efforts. Are you meeting your goals? Adjust your strategy based on what works and what doesn't. Use successful interactions to determine where you might need to improve. A journal or an app can help track your engagement with each community. Note the value you provide and receive, and reflect on how these interactions contribute to your growth.

Note that building your network is a dynamic process. But if you're strategic and sincere, you'll strengthen your professional community and open doors to new opportunities.

**Summing It Up**

The Community Revolution is all about building strong, supportive networks and engaging with our communities. You can enhance personal and professional growth through the connections you form, contribute to collective success, and leave a lasting impact.

# Key Takeaways

• Building and nurturing high-value networks is crucial for personal and professional growth.
• Engaging actively in community activities provides support, accountability, and opportunities for learning and collaboration.
• Providing value to your community strengthens connections and fosters collaboration.
• The Community Revolution is about leveraging collective effort to achieve individual and communal goals.

**Looking Ahead**

As we continue our journey through the Community Revolution, the next chapter will focus on giving back and creating a legacy. This essential step will help you understand how to make a lasting impact and contribute to your community and industry, ensuring you leave a meaningful legacy.

# Chapter 11:
## Leveraging Networks for Growth

Are you familiar with the saying that one's network is their net worth? This saying rings even truer when you consider the nature of today's work environment. A strong, high-value network can offer you all the support, resources, and opportunities you need to thrive personally and professionally. In this chapter, we will explore the importance of building and leveraging networks, strategies for effective networking, and the role of financial discipline and diversifying income streams in achieving long-term success.

To begin, let's talk about the importance of networks and how they can be leveraged for personal and professional growth.

## The Importance of Networks

Networks are crucial for career growth and personal development. They provide access to information, opportunities, mentorship, and support, all vital for navigating the complexities of modern careers. According to a study by LinkedIn, 85% of jobs are filled through networking. This illuminates the critical role of networks in career advancement.

A network is like a keychain full of different keys. Each key represents a connection with unique access to various opportunities and resources. Just as you would use the right key to open a specific lock, you use different relationships in your network to unlock doors to new job prospects, advice, or collaborations. The more keys you have and know how to use, the better you can navigate and open doors in your career.

So, leveraging your network means using your relationships and connections to achieve your personal or professional goals. It involves:

- Tap into the expertise, advice, and information your contacts can provide.
- Use your network to uncover job openings, project collaborations, or business opportunities you might not have found on your own.
- Getting recommendations, endorsements, or moral support from your connections. This could mean a mentor offering guidance or a colleague vouching for you professionally.

In my personal life, I train at a local CrossFit gym with other entrepreneurial dads from various industries, such as real estate, finance, nutrition, and tattooing. This community keeps me accountable and helps me build habits that enhance my personal growth. Professionally, I am a member of a strategic innovation advisory board where I contribute thought leadership, run workshops and lead discussions with peers. Additionally, I participate in curated social communities focused on building friendships and value networks among Black executive men. These networks have been instrumental in my growth, providing diverse perspectives and opportunities.

## Strategies for Leveraging Networks

Your network can be categorized into two:

1. **Personal Networks**: These include friends, family, and acquaintances. They can offer emotional support, share advice, and even provide leads on job opportunities or projects. Personal connections can often introduce you to their professional networks, expanding your reach.

2. **Professional Networks**: These consist of colleagues, mentors, industry contacts, and other professionals you've met through work-related events or platforms. They can offer career guidance, industry insights, and potential job opportunities. They're also useful for professional growth through workshops, seminars, and conferences.

Integrating both networks to create a robust support system is key to effective leverage. For example, a personal connection might recommend you for a job opening they heard about through their own professional network. Or a professional contact might provide personal advice on handling work-life balance.

Here's how to leverage your network effectively:

For Personal Growth:

**1. Seek Advice and Feedback**
- Action: Reach out to your network for advice on personal projects or challenges.
- Example: "Hey [Name], I'm improving my public speaking skills. Can you share any tips or resources?"

**2. Find Accountability Partners**
- Action: Partner with someone in your network to keep each other accountable for personal goals.
- Example: "Hi [Name], I aim to run a marathon next year. Would you be interested in being my accountability partner?"

**3. Join or Form Interest Groups**
- Action: Join groups or communities within your network that align with your interests.
- Example: "I noticed a few colleagues are into photography. Would you be interested in forming a photography club?"

**4. Access Resources**

- Action: Utilize the expertise and resources of your network for personal projects.
- Example: "Do you have any book recommendations on mindfulness?"

For Professional Growth:

## 1. Career Advice and Mentorship
- Action: Seek career advice or mentorship from experienced professionals in your network.
- Example: "Can we have a coffee chat? I'd love to get your insights on advancing in my career."

## 2. Job Referrals
- Action: Let your network know when you seek new job opportunities.
- Example: "I'm exploring new opportunities in digital marketing. Do you know of any openings, or can you refer me to someone in that field?"

## 3. Collaborate on Projects
- Action: Propose collaborations on professional projects or side gigs.
- Example: "I'm working on a new app idea. Would you be interested in collaborating?"

## 4. Professional Development
- Action: Ask for recommendations on courses, seminars, or certifications.
- Example: "I'm looking to improve my data analysis skills. Do you have any course recommendations?"

## 5. Expand Your Knowledge

- Action: Engage in discussions and share knowledge within your network.
- Example: "I read an interesting article on blockchain technology. What are your thoughts on its future applications?"

### 6. Access Hidden Opportunities
- Action: Tap into the hidden job market through your network.
- Example: "I'm interested in roles that might not be publicly advertised. Do you know of any opportunities?"

### 7. Professional Endorsements and Recommendations
- Action: Request endorsements or recommendations on professional platforms.
- Example: "Could you write a LinkedIn recommendation for me based on our work together?"

### 8. Gain New Perspectives
- Action: Get diverse perspectives on professional challenges.
- Example: "I'm facing a challenge at work. Can we brainstorm some solutions?"

Use these tips to effectively leverage your network for growth in all aspects of life.

### Summing It Up

As a professional, leveraging networks for growth is essential. So, get to work and identify the networks that offer the most value, engage authentically with others, and take advantage of opportunities that come your way. This approach will boost your personal and professional development.

# Key Takeaways

- Building and leveraging high-value networks is crucial for career growth and personal development.

- Engaging authentically in your networks can lead to meaningful relationships and new opportunities.
- Financial discipline and diversifying income streams are essential for achieving long-term freedom and stability.

## Looking Ahead

As we continue our journey through the Community Revolution, the next chapter will focus on giving back and creating a legacy. It will help you understand how to make a lasting impact and contribute to your community and industry, ensuring you leave a meaningful legacy.

# Chapter 12:
## Giving Back and Creating a Legacy

Imagine planting a tree. When you first plant it, you might enjoy the shade or a few fruits it produces, but over time, that tree grows stronger and larger. It provides shade for others, fruits for future generations, and a home for birds and insects. Giving back is like planting that tree. You might see immediate benefits when you contribute to your community, but the actual impact is seen over time.

Creating a legacy works in the same way. Just as a tree continues to give long after it's planted, your efforts to help others create a lasting effect that benefits future generations. Isn't that what we all want? To leave the world a bit better than we found it? When you give back, you plant seeds of change that can grow and thrive, providing support and inspiration for years.

As we continue our journey through the Community Revolution, it's essential to understand the profound impact of giving back and creating a lasting legacy. Giving back to your community benefits others and enriches your life, enhancing your sense of purpose and fulfillment.

This chapter focuses on how you can make meaningful contributions, the importance of legacy, and practical steps to leave a lasting impact.

### The Importance of Giving Back

Giving back and creating a lasting impact is more than just a nice thing– it's essential for personal fulfillment and community growth. When you contribute your skills, knowledge, or resources to causes you care about, you're helping others and enriching your life. It's a way to make a real difference in the world and leave a positive legacy.

When you give back, you nurture a sense of belonging and purpose. Giving back allows you to contribute to the well-being of others, creating a positive ripple effect that can inspire and uplift entire communities.

According to the Corporation for National and Community Service, individuals who volunteer regularly experience lower mortality rates, greater functional ability, and lower rates of depression later in life.

I have witnessed the transformative power of giving back throughout my career and personal life. Inspired by the legacies of our ancestors, including that of my wife's grandfather, Seth Anthony, who, as I said before, played a significant role in Ghana's journey to independence, my wife and I started a family business and foundation. Named after our fathers and grandfathers, we aim to impact others through affordable housing, financial literacy, and life-skills education to help the less fortunate activate life-work revolutions. This initiative is a tribute to our ancestors and a legacy for our daughters to build upon.

Growing up in one of the poorest congressional districts in New York City during the 80s and 90s, I saw firsthand the challenges of poverty and the struggle to succeed. Although I was fortunate not to experience housing instability, thanks to my family, I was surrounded by environments that were not conducive to success. Many families from marginalized communities face lower wages and must work longer hours in lower-skilled jobs, making it challenging to make ends meet. We desire to give others a fair chance by caring for core needs like housing and marketable skills to earn decent wages.

## How to Give Back and Create a Lasting Impact

The good news is that you can approach giving back in many practical ways. Here are some tips to get started immediately:

**1. Share Your Skills**: Think about what you're good at and how to use those skills to benefit others. Whether you're a financial advisor, a tech expert, or a healthcare professional, you can offer pro bono services, mentor someone, or provide training. Sharing your expertise can significantly impact someone's career or personal development.

**2. Volunteer Your Time**: Commit to a cause that resonates with you. Volunteering doesn't always mean a long-term commitment; even a few hours a month can be impactful. Look for local organizations or charities that align with your interests and skills. It's a great way to contribute directly to your community.

**3. Mentorship and Coaching**: Offer to mentor someone who could benefit from your experience. Whether it's a young professional starting or someone looking to make a career change, your guidance can provide invaluable support and insight.

**4. Donate Wisely**: Financial contributions can go a long way. Research charities and nonprofit organizations to ensure that your donations are used effectively. Consider setting up a recurring donation if you're able to. Even small, regular contributions can add up to significant support.

**5. Get Involved in Community Projects**: Participate in or organize community events or initiatives. This could be anything from local clean-up days to fundraising events for a cause you care about. Engaging with your community can help address local needs and build a stronger, more connected environment.

**6. Advocate for Causes**: Use your voice to advocate for causes you believe in. This might involve speaking at events, writing articles, or raising awareness through social media. Advocacy can help drive change and encourage others to get involved as well.

143

**7. Build Partnerships**: Collaborate with others who share your goals. Partnering with like-minded individuals or organizations can amplify your efforts and create a more significant impact. Combining resources and expertise often leads to more effective outcomes.

**8. Support Education**: Invest in education by supporting scholarships, funding educational programs, or mentoring students. Education can be a powerful tool for change, and your support can open doors for those who may not have had the opportunity otherwise.

Remember, the key is to choose areas where your contributions will have the most effect. It's not just about giving back; it's about meaningfully and strategically. So, think about what matters and how to leverage your professional skills to make a real difference. Your efforts can have a lasting and profound impact, no matter how small they may seem.

### Practical Exercise: Creating Your Legacy

Creating a legacy might seem daunting, but it doesn't have to be. This simple exercise will give you a clearer vision of the legacy you want to leave behind and some concrete steps to start building it.

### Step 1: Define Your Legacy

**Question**: What do you want to be remembered for?

Take a moment to reflect on your core values. What drives you? What are you passionate about? Write down a few keywords that represent these values.

**Examples**: Integrity, kindness, innovation, teaching, and resilience.

### Step 2: Identify Your Impact Areas

**Question**: Where do you want to make an impact?

Consider different areas of your life: family, work, community, or a specific cause. Write down where you want to make a difference.

**Example**: Family – being a supportive and loving parent, Work – mentoring young professionals, Community – volunteering at local shelters.

### Step 3: Set Specific Goals

**Question**: What specific goals can you set to start building your legacy?

Break down your impact areas into actionable goals. Be specific about what you want to achieve and how you plan to do it.

**Example**:

- Family: Spend one hour each evening with my children without any distractions.
- Work: Mentor at least two interns annually and help them develop their careers.
- Community: Volunteer at the local shelter every Saturday morning.

### Step 4: Take Action

**Question**: What can you do today to start working towards your goals?

Identify immediate actions you can take. Building a legacy is a continuous process, so focus on consistency.

**Example**:

- Tonight, turn off your phone during family time.
- Tomorrow, schedule a meeting with your interns to discuss their goals and how you can help.
- This Saturday, show up at the shelter and offer your time and skills.

### Step 5: Share Your Story

**Question**: How can you inspire others with your journey?

Sharing your experiences can motivate others to think about their own legacies. Talk about your journey with friends, family or through social media.

**Example**: Write a blog post about the joys and challenges of mentoring or share a story about a memorable volunteering experience.

Creating your legacy isn't about grand gestures or fame. It's about living in a way that reflects your values and positively impacts those around you. Start one step at a time today, and watch your legacy take shape.

### Summing It Up

Giving back and creating a legacy is fundamental to the Life-Work Revolution. By contributing your time, resources, and skills to your community, you can make a lasting impact that benefits both you and others.

## Key Takeaways

- Giving back fosters a sense of purpose and fulfillment.
- Identify your passions and strengths to find meaningful ways to contribute.
- Set clear goals and intentions for your community involvement.
- Engage with local communities and leverage your professional skills to benefit others.
- Building a legacy involves creating long-term initiatives and documenting your journey.
- Financial discipline and diversifying income streams are essential for long-term freedom and the ability to thrive beyond the 9 to 5.

### Looking Ahead

In the final chapter of this part, we will be looking at how you can adopt the financial FREEDOM model to create the life you desire and acquire the resources necessary to support your purpose. Remember that financial freedom isn't just about wealth. It's about aligning your financial habits and strategies with your long-term goals and values. The FREEDOM model is the best tool to guide you in this pursuit.

# Chapter 13:
## Financial Freedom: Hiring Your Money to Work for You

Achieving financial freedom is vital to the Life-Work Revolution. It's about more than just managing money. You have to reclaim your time, create opportunities, and ultimately design a life that aligns with your values and aspirations. My journey, which began from humble beginnings, has been shaped by trial and error, building high value skills, networks, and applying life-work design principles to achieve financial flexibility and independence. This chapter introduces the FREEDOM model – a unique framework I've developed to help you navigate your own path to financial independence while also integrating the levels of financial freedom that mark milestones along this journey.

**Understanding the Levels of Financial Freedom**

The pathway to financial freedom can be visualized through six levels or stages, each representing a milestone that brings you closer to living life and doing work on your own terms. These levels build upon one another, offering a clear roadmap for how you can progress from financial instability to financial abundance.

**1. Level 1: Solvency**

Achieving solvency is the crucial first step toward financial freedom. Solvency means your income consistently covers essential living expenses – housing, food, utilities, transportation, and healthcare – without relying on debt. It forms the foundation for all future financial growth.

Start by assessing your income and expenses. If you're spending more than you earn, make adjustments by cutting non-essential costs, like dining out or unused subscriptions, and reallocating funds to necessities. Consider increasing your income through a side gig, raise, or better-paying job.

Budgeting is key. Create a plan that prioritizes covering basic expenses and paying down high-interest debt. As you regain control of your finances, you'll reduce stress and gain more space to think long-term.

When I started, solvency was my focus. Managing my expenses and creating stability allowed me to lay the groundwork for future success.

## 2. Level 2: Stability

Stability is achieved when you consistently save a portion of your income, creating a buffer for unexpected expenses. At this stage, you're no longer just breaking even but building a financial cushion that helps you avoid falling back into debt. Stability allows you to focus on long-term planning without the constant fear of financial emergencies.

The first priority is to build an emergency fund that covers 3-6 months of essential living expenses. Start by setting aside small, manageable amounts regularly, even if it's just a few dollars each week. Automate this process, so saving becomes a habit, and gradually increase contributions as your financial situation improves.

Creating an emergency fund was a critical step in my journey. It provided the peace of mind needed to focus on long-term growth rather than day-to-day survival.

## 3. Level 3: Bad Debt Freedom

At this level, the focus shifts to eliminating bad debt, freeing up resources to begin building sustainable wealth. Bad debt – such as credit card debt or high-interest personal loans – drains your income and prevents you from making financial progress. Paying off these liabilities reduces your financial burden and gives you the freedom to invest in your future.

Start by implementing a bad debt repayment strategy. Focus on paying off high-interest debts first, as they accrue the most cost over time. You can use methods like the avalanche approach (targeting the highest interest rates first) or the snowball method (paying off the smallest debts first). Once you've cleared this financial drag, redirect the money you would have used for debt payments into savings or investments that grow your wealth.

Becoming bad debt-free was a major turning point in my life. It allowed me to redirect money towards investments that would grow my wealth rather than servicing liability driven loans.

### 4. Level 4: Security

Financial security means that your investments or passive income can cover your basic survival expenses. It's a significant step toward financial independence, as you are no longer fully reliant on active income to survive.

To reach financial security, focus on diversifying your investments to generate multiple streams of passive income. This could include dividend-paying stocks, rental properties, bonds, or even a side business. The key is to ensure that the income from these sources is stable and sufficient to meet your basic needs. The more diversified your income, the more resilient you'll be against market fluctuations or economic downturns.

Achieving financial security was empowering. Knowing that my basic needs were covered gave me the freedom to take calculated risks in my career and investments.

## 5. Level 5: Independence

You reach this level when your passive income can cover all of your living expenses, freeing you from the need to work for money. Financial independence represents a significant achievement, as you gain the freedom to choose how you spend your time without the constraints of a traditional job.

To achieve and maintain financial independence, continue to grow and optimize your investments. Focus on diversifying and reinvesting your income streams to ensure they remain robust and capable of sustaining your lifestyle. Consider exploring new opportunities, such as real estate, stocks, or even entrepreneurial ventures that can generate additional passive income. Regularly assess your portfolio to make adjustments based on market conditions and your evolving goals.

Reaching financial independence was the realization of a long-term goal. It allows me to redirect my focus on passion projects and giving back to the community in ways that expand my legacy.

## 6. Level 6: Abundance

Abundance is the final level, where your investment income significantly exceeds your living expenses, allowing you to pursue any project or passion without financial constraints. This leaves room for greater creativity and fulfillment in your endeavors.

With abundance in hand, shift your focus toward legacy-building activities. This can include mentoring others to help them achieve their financial goals, starting philanthropic ventures that address community needs, or investing in local initiatives that nurture growth and opportunity. Channeling your resources into meaningful projects means you can create a positive impact that extends beyond your own life.

Today, I'm striving towards abundance – not just for myself, but to create opportunities for others. It's about leaving a legacy that reflects my values and aspirations.

**The FREEDOM Model**

The FREEDOM model is a guiding framework designed to help you structure your approach to financial freedom. It emphasizes the mindset, behaviors, and disciplined actions necessary to build and sustain financial independence. This model aligns with the principles of the Life-Work Revolution, particularly the Community Revolution, where financial freedom empowers you to give back, create a legacy, and contribute to the broader community.

1. **F** – Focus on High-Value Skills

2. **R** – Reinvest in Growth

3. **E** – Establish Multiple Income Streams

4. **E** – Eliminate Debt Strategically

5. **D** – Design an Automated Financial System

6. **O** – Optimize Investments for Long-Term Growth

7. **M** – Maximize Tax Efficiency

**Personal Example: Applying the FREEDOM Model**

In my journey toward financial independence, the FREEDOM model has been instrumental. For instance, I focus on leveraging my expertise in building skills-based organizations (SBO) by offering advisory services at a premium rate. This side income allows me to invest in other ventures, including real estate and digital products, which generate passive income. By automating my financial systems and maximizing tax efficiency, I've created a sustainable financial plan that supports my long-term goals and legacy-building efforts. This approach has allowed me to fund family initiatives and contribute meaningfully to the communities I care about.

| FREEDOM Component | Overview | Action | Result |
|---|---|---|---|
| **Focus on High-Value Skills** | Leverage unique skills to create income streams. | Offered advisory services in building skills-based organizations (SBO) at a premium rate. | Generated significant side income to reinvest in other ventures. |
| **Reinvest in Growth** | Continuously invest in personal and professional development. | Allocated earnings from advisory services to further education and certifications. | Enhanced expertise, leading to higher advisory fees and new opportunities. |
| **Establish Multiple Income Streams** | Diversify income sources to build financial security. | Invested in real estate and digital products generating passive income. | Created sustainable passive income, reducing reliance on primary job. |
| **Eliminate Bad Debt Strategically** | Focus on eliminating high-interest bad debt to increase financial freedom. | Paid down high-interest bad debt using income from side ventures and strategic budgeting. | Reduced bad debt burden, freeing up more income for investments and savings. |
| **Design an Automated Financial System** | Automate financial processes to ensure consistency. | Set up automated transfers to savings, investments, and bill payments. | Maintained consistent financial growth with minimal effort. |

| FREEDOM Component | Overview | Action | Result |
|---|---|---|---|
| Optimize Investments for Long-Term Growth | Maximize returns through strategic investment choices. | Invested in tax-advantaged accounts and diversified across asset classes. | Achieved long-term financial growth and stability. |
| Maximize Tax Efficiency | Utilize tax strategies to retain more earnings. | Leveraged tax-advantaged accounts and efficient investment vehicles. | Reduced tax liabilities, increasing overall wealth accumulation. |

Keep in mind that financial freedom is a cornerstone of the Community Revolution within the Life-Work Revolution framework. By achieving financial independence, you not only secure your future but also create the capacity to contribute to your community, mentor others, and build a lasting legacy. The FREEDOM model provides a structured approach to achieving this, ensuring that your financial resources align with your broader life and work goals.

**Summing It Up**

The FREEDOM model offers a roadmap for achieving financial independence by focusing on high-value skills, reinvesting in growth, establishing multiple income streams, and optimizing financial management. By adopting these principles, you empower yourself to live a life of purpose and impact, free from the constraints of financial insecurity.

# Key Takeaways

• The FREEDOM model integrates with the Life-Work Revolution, providing a structured approach to financial independence.

- High-value skills and multiple income streams are essential for building financial freedom.

- Strategic debt elimination, automation, and tax efficiency are critical components of a sustainable financial plan.

- Financial freedom empowers you to contribute to your community and build a legacy.

**Looking Ahead**

That's it – congratulations on concluding your journey through the Community Revolution. We've explored the three aspects of the Life-Work Revolution: Internal, External, and Community.

Now, in the final part of this book, I will show you how to synthesize everything you've learned into a personalized life-work revolution strategy. This final step will ensure you are equipped to continue your journey towards achieving your personal and professional goals, whether short-term or long-term.

Let's get into it!

# Part 5:
## Creating Your Personalized Life-Work Revolution Plan

Do you ever wonder why some "expert" advice doesn't seem to fit no matter what you do? Well, that is because we all live a unique life. You and I are two different individuals; therefore, we can't follow the same path in life. As such, everything you've learned throughout this book is only meant to guide you through creating your personalized life-work revolution plan.

Why is this important?

A personalized life-work revolution plan is essential because it aligns with your individual needs, goals, and circumstances. We all have different priorities. What matters most to you might differ completely from what matters to your colleague or friend. Personalizing your plan ensures that your most important aspects – family, career, or personal growth – get the attention they deserve.

Another reason is that generic goals often fail to inspire or motivate. When your plan is tailored to your specific aspirations, you're more likely to set meaningful and attainable goals. This personal touch makes your objectives more relevant and achievable.

Plus, life is unpredictable. A one-size-fits-all plan doesn't account for the unexpected changes and challenges you might face. Meanwhile, a personalized plan can be adapted and adjusted without losing sight of your long-term goals.

Finally, you're more likely to stick with a plan that resonates with you on a personal level. Staying motivated and committed is more accessible when the plan concerns your life and aspirations. Personal relevance drives engagement and persistence.

The point is that creating a personalized life-work revolution plan ensures that every aspect of your journey is tailored to fit you perfectly. This approach enhances your chances of success and makes the entire process more meaningful and enjoyable.

So, if you're ready to start crafting your plan, let's dive into the next chapter.

# Chapter 14:
## Applying Design Thinking to Your Life

Have you ever wondered why some solutions just click while others miss the mark? The secret often lies in two powerful approaches: Design and Systems Thinking. These methodologies can transform the way we tackle problems and create innovations.

**Design Thinking**: Design Thinking is all about empathy. It puts you in the user's shoes (in this case, you), helping you understand their needs, challenges, and desires. Why is this important? Because solutions that resonate with people are more likely to succeed.

**Systems Thinking**: While Design Thinking zeroes in on the user, Systems Thinking zooms out to see the bigger picture. It's about understanding how different system parts interact and influence each other. Think of it as mapping the whole ecosystem.

## Steps to Create Your Life-Work Revolution Strategy

Design and Systems thinking are powerful methodologies that can be leveraged to create a personalized life-work revolution strategy. Doing this can be incredibly beneficial as both approaches focus on empathy, experimentation, and holistic understanding, which enables you to design a life that aligns with your values and aspirations.

Here's how to apply them to your life-work revolution plan:

### 1. Empathize with Yourself

Start by understanding your own needs, aspirations, and challenges. Conduct a self-audit of your values, passions, strengths, and areas for growth. Then, take some time to reflect on your experiences. What are your pain points? What brings you joy and fulfillment?

## 2. Define Your Goals

Based on your self-reflection, clearly define your long-term goals that align with your vision. What will you achieve in the next 5, 10, or 20 years? Defining your goals helps you stay focused and gives you a direction to work towards. When setting your goals, use the SMART criteria (Specific, Measurable, Achievable, Relevant, Time-bound).

## 3. Ideate Potential Solutions

Brainstorm different ways to achieve your goals. Think outside the box and explore all possible paths. What are the different career options, lifestyle changes, or learning opportunities available to you?

## 4. Prototype and Experiment

Create simple action plans that you can test and adjust as you go. Opt for a low-risk experiment. For example, if considering a career change, take on a freelance project in a new field.

## 5. Test and Reflect

Implement your prototypes, gather feedback, and reflect on the outcomes. What worked well? What didn't? How can you improve your approach? Use this information to iterate and improve your strategy.

This integrated approach helps you create a long-term life-work revolution plan that is user-centric and system-aware. It ensures that your actions are aligned with your goals and that you are adaptable to changes and new insights along the way.

## Personal Experience

I use design thinking principles regularly to navigate career transitions and achieve my goals. It's safe to say it's a staple in my toolkit. Here's how I have applied these steps:

- **Empathize**: I reflected on my values and realized my passion for helping others improve their skills.
- **Define**: I set a goal to become a thought leader in life-work design.
- **Ideate**: I brainstormed various ways to achieve this, including writing a book, speaking at conferences, and offering coaching services.
- **Prototype**: I started by writing blog posts and giving free workshops to test my ideas.
- **Test and Reflect**: I gathered feedback from participants and refined my approach, eventually leading to the creation of the Life-Work Revolution.

## Creating Your Personalized Life-Work Revolution Strategy

This book provides the tools, principles, and methodologies to create a personalized life-work revolution strategy. However, engaging my services can further support you in building and executing this strategy, ensuring you achieve life-work synergy.

### Benefits of a Personalized Strategy

- **Clarity and Direction**: Understand your values, goals, and the steps needed to achieve them.
- **Alignment**: Ensure that your personal and professional lives are aligned with your core values and aspirations.
- **Adaptability**: Develop a flexible strategy that can adapt to changes and challenges.
- **Support and Accountability**: Receive ongoing support and accountability to stay on track and achieve your goals.

**Engaging My Services**

• **One-on-One Coaching**: Personalized coaching sessions to help you navigate your life-work revolution.

• **Workshops and Webinars**: Interactive sessions on design, systems thinking, and life-work synergy.

• **Resources and Tools**: Access to exclusive resources, templates, and tools to support your journey.

• **Community Support**: Join a community of like-minded individuals on their life-work revolution journey.

Brooks engaged in my one-on-one coaching services to develop his personalized life-work revolution strategy. Thanks to our sessions, he gained clarity on his goals, created a flexible plan, and received ongoing support to navigate challenges and stay on track.

## Practical Steps for Applying Design Thinking

Below are more practical steps for applying design thinking:

• **Empathy Mapping**: Creating an empathy map can help deeply understand your needs, feelings, and motivations. Divide a paper into four sections: "Say," "Think," "Feel," and "Do." Reflect on what you say, think, feel, and do in different contexts to understand your needs and desires.

• **Journey Mapping**: Map out your current journey to identify pain points and opportunities for improvement. Create a timeline of your typical day or week. Note down activities, emotions, and any challenges you face. Identify areas where you can make positive changes.

• **Brainstorming Sessions**: Conduct brainstorming sessions to generate various ideas and solutions. For instance, set a timer for 15 minutes and write down as many ideas as possible for achieving one of your goals. Don't judge or filter the ideas—just let them flow.

• **Prototyping Experiments**: Develop small-scale prototypes to test your ideas in real-world settings. Choose one idea from your brainstorming session and create a simple prototype or experiment to test it. For example, if you want to explore a new career, take an online course or volunteer in that field.

- **Reflective Journaling**: Set aside time each week to journal about your experiments, what you learned, and how you can improve your approach. Use this reflection to iterate and refine your strategy.

### Summing It Up

Applying design and systems thinking to your life can help you create a personalized life-work revolution strategy. Designing a life that aligns with your values and aspirations is possible once you understand your needs, set clear goals, ideate solutions, prototype experiments, and monitor your progress.

## Key Takeaways

- Design and systems thinking are powerful methodologies for creating a personalized life-work revolution strategy.
- Engaging with my services can provide additional support, resources, and accountability to help you achieve life-work synergy.
- Practical tools and exercises, such as empathy mapping, journey mapping, brainstorming sessions, prototyping experiments, and reflective journaling, can guide you in designing your strategy.

### Looking Ahead

As we get closer to the end of our journey, the next chapter will focus on building effective habits. Developing and maintaining beneficial habits is essential for sustaining progress and achieving your life-work revolution goals.

# Chapter 15:
## Building Effective Habits

You need effective habits to maintain progress and achieve your long-term life-work revolution goals. This chapter explores the science of habit formation and introduces a proprietary framework to help you develop and sustain beneficial habits. Understanding and leveraging the habit formation loop—cue, routine, and reward—can help you build and break old habits.

For example, Brooks wanted to improve his daily productivity. Once he identified his morning tea as a cue, he added a routine of planning his day right after his first sip and rewarded himself with a brief walk outside. This simple habit significantly improved his focus and efficiency throughout the day.

### Introducing the SPARC Framework

To help you develop and maintain effective habits, I have created the SPARC Framework. SPARC stands for Set, Plan, Act, Reflect, and Celebrate. This framework is designed to guide you through the process of building and sustaining habits that align with your life-work revolution goals.

- **S – Set Your Intentions**: Clearly define and write down the habit you want to build. Ensure it aligns with your values and goals. Make it actionable.
- **P – Plan Your Routine**: Establish the specific actions you will take to build your habit. Identify the cue that will trigger your habit, your routine, and the reward you will give yourself.
- **A – Act Consistently**: Consistency is key to habit formation. Commit to performing your habit daily for at least 21 days. Use a habit tracker to monitor your progress.

- **R – Reflect on Your Progress**: Regularly review your habit formation journey. Set aside time each week to journal about your habits. Note your successes, challenges, and any adjustments needed.
- **C – Celebrate Your Wins**: Celebrating your achievements reinforces your habits and motivates you to continue. Identify meaningful rewards for reaching milestones. Acknowledge your progress and reflect on how far you've come.

In my journey, building effective habits has been essential for maintaining my productivity and well-being. Here's how I have applied the SPARC Framework:

- **Set**: I wanted to improve my morning productivity by starting my day with a clear plan.
- **Plan**: I used my morning workout as a cue to plan my day. After my workout, I spent 10 minutes journaling my tasks and priorities.
- **Act**: I committed to this routine every morning for 21 days, using a habit tracker to monitor my progress.
- **Reflect**: I reviewed my journal each week to see what was working and made adjustments.
- **Celebrate**: After consistently following my routine for a month, and I enjoyed a weekend getaway to celebrate my improved productivity.

### Client Examples and Results

### Example 1: Sarah's Networking Habit

- **Set**: Sarah wanted to build a habit of professional networking to expand her career opportunities.
- **Plan**: She decided to use her morning coffee as a cue to send one LinkedIn message to a new connection each day.
- **Act**: Sarah consistently sent a message every morning for 30 days.

- **Reflect**: She tracked her progress and noted increased positive responses and networking opportunities.
- **Celebrate**: Sarah rewarded herself with a professional development course after completing her 30-day networking challenge.

### Example 2: Reggie's Learning Habit

- **Set**: Reggie aimed to develop a habit of continuous learning to stay ahead in his field.
- **Plan**: He used his lunch break as a cue to read an industry-related article or watch a short educational video.
- **Act**: Reggie maintained this routine daily for two months.
- **Reflect**: He kept a log of what he learned and how it applied to his work, noticing significant improvements in his knowledge and skills.
- **Celebrate**: Reggie celebrated his new habit by attending a relevant industry conference.

### Example 3: Emily's Fitness Habit

- **Set**: Emily wanted to incorporate regular exercise into her daily routine.
- **Plan**: She set her alarm 30 minutes earlier and used it as a cue to start her day with a yoga session.
- **Act**: Emily followed this routine every morning for three months.
- **Reflect**: She tracked her progress and noted improvements in her physical and mental well-being.
- **Celebrate**: Emily rewarded herself with a new yoga mat and outfit after three consistent months.

## Practical Tools for Habit Formation

Here are some of my favorite tools for forming new habits:

**1. Habit Stacking**: Link a new habit to an existing one. This method leverages the existing habit's established cue and routine to support the new habit. If you already drink coffee in the morning, add a new habit, like reading a book for 10 minutes immediately after your first sip.

**2. Implementation Intentions**: Create a specific plan that outlines when, where, and how you will perform the new habit. This helps increase the likelihood of following through. For example, "I will meditate for 10 minutes in my living room at 7 AM every morning."

**3. Temptation Bundling**: Pair a habit you need to do with a habit you want to do. This makes the necessary habit more enjoyable and increases your motivation to complete it. For example, only listen to your favorite podcast while working out.

**4. Visual Cues**: Use visual reminders to prompt you to perform your new habit. These cues can help you stay focused and on track. For instance, you might place a book on your bedside table to remind you to read before bed.

Research shows that habits are stored in the basal ganglia, a part of the brain that forms routines and repetitive behaviors. This explains why habits, once established, become automatic and require less cognitive effort to perform.

Additionally, some studies indicate that positive reinforcement is more effective than punishment in establishing new habits. Rewards are positively associated with the behavior, increasing the likelihood of repetition.

Research by BJ Fogg, a behavior scientist, suggests consistency is more important than intensity when forming new habits. Small, consistent actions are more sustainable and lead to long-term habit formation.

## Practical Exercise: Creating a Habit Plan

You only need these five steps to create your habit plan:

**1. Choose a Habit**: Pick a habit you want to develop or change. Start with something simple and specific. Got one in mind? Great! Write it down to make it clear and actionable.

**2. Identify Cues and Rewards**: What will trigger your habit? What reward will you give yourself for sticking to it? Write down the cue that will prompt your habit and the reward you'll use to keep yourself motivated.

**3. Set Up a Routine**: Create a routine that you can easily follow. Outline the steps you'll take to perform your habit. Keep it simple and repeatable.

**4. Track Your Progress**: Use a habit tracker to monitor how you're doing. Create or download one, and use it daily to note your successes and areas for improvement.

**5. Reflect and Adjust**: Set aside time each week to review your habit plan. What's working? What needs to change? Make the necessary adjustments to keep improving.

These steps are practical and straightforward, which makes them easy to implement.

### Summing It Up

Building effective habits is essential for sustaining your life-work revolution. By understanding the science of habit formation and using practical tools and strategies, you can develop and maintain habits that support your goals.

## Key Takeaways

- Effective habits are built through understanding cues, routines, and rewards.
- The SPARC Framework (Set, Plan, Act, Reflect, Celebrate) provides a structured approach to habit formation.
- Practical tools like habit stacking, implementation intentions, and temptation bundling can help establish new habits.

- Consistency and positive reinforcement are crucial for long-term habit formation.
- Regular reflection and adjustment ensure your habits remain effective and aligned with your goals.

**Looking Ahead**

The next chapter will focus on maintaining momentum and overcoming challenges. You will learn strategies to stay motivated and resilient as you continue your life-work revolution journey.

# Chapter 16:
## Maintaining Momentum and Overcoming Challenges

At the beginning of a new plan, the initial excitement propels you into thinking nothing can stop you now. But once a plan is executed, the real challenge lies in maintaining momentum and overcoming inevitable obstacles. This chapter explores strategies for staying on track, overcoming challenges, and sustaining your progress over the long term.

### Why is staying on track difficult?

Maintaining momentum and motivation when following a long-term plan is undoubtedly challenging. Several factors contribute to this difficulty, so understanding why momentum and motivation wane and how to address these issues is essential.

Firstly, the initial excitement of starting a new project or plan often wanes over time. At the beginning of any endeavor, there is a surge of enthusiasm and optimism. This initial boost is a powerful motivator, propelling you forward with energy and determination. However, as time progresses, this excitement naturally diminishes. The novelty wears off, and the plan transitions from an exciting challenge to a routine task. This shift can lead to feelings of disillusionment and a lack of enthusiasm.

Secondly, the lack of immediate results can significantly impact motivation. In a world where instant gratification is highly valued, long-term plans often require sustained effort before yielding noticeable results. The absence of quick wins can lead to frustration and impatience. When progress is not immediately visible, it is easy to feel like the efforts are in vain, causing motivation to plummet.

The question, "Why am I doing this?" may arise frequently, leading to a reassessment of the plan's worth.

Daily distractions are another major obstacle in maintaining momentum. Life is full of unexpected events and responsibilities that can derail focus and commitment. Work demands, family obligations, and unforeseen circumstances can interrupt the continuity of a long-term plan. These distractions can make it challenging to stay on track and maintain the consistent effort required to achieve your long-term goals. When constantly pulled in different directions, it becomes difficult to prioritize and allocate sufficient time and energy to the plan.

Furthermore, the monotony of repetitive tasks can sap motivation. Long-term plans often involve routine activities that need to be performed regularly. The repetitive nature of these tasks can lead to boredom and a sense of struggle. Without variety and excitement, it becomes harder to stay engaged and motivated. The feeling of merely going through the motions can diminish the sense of purpose and passion initially felt.

Self-doubt is also a significant factor that can erode motivation. As time passes, one may start to question their abilities and the feasibility of their goals. This self-doubt can be crippling, leading to a lack of confidence and a diminished belief in the plan's success. The nagging thought, "Can I really do this?" can undermine efforts and create a negative feedback loop, where decreased motivation leads to decreased effort, further diminishing results.

Lastly, long-term plans often involve overwhelming tasks. The sheer scale of the goals can be intimidating and cause anxiety. When faced with a large, seemingly impossible task, it is easy to feel overwhelmed and paralyzed. The perception that the goal is too big to handle can lead to procrastination and avoidance, further stalling progress.

Given these, how can you stay on track with the life-work revolution no matter what?

## Strategies for Staying on Track

Adopting specific strategies to overcome these challenges and maintain momentum and motivation.

**1. Create a Schedule**: Develop a detailed schedule or timeline that includes when and how you'll tackle each step. Use a planner or digital calendar to set reminders and keep yourself accountable.

**2. Monitor Your Progress**: Regularly check how you're doing against your schedule. Update your progress and make adjustments if necessary. This helps you stay on course and see how far you've come.

**3. Stay Organized**: Keep your workspace and materials organized. An organized environment can reduce stress and distractions, making it easier to focus on your tasks.

**4. Manage Distractions**: Identify what typically distracts you and develop strategies to minimize these interruptions. This might involve setting specific times for focused work or creating a dedicated workspace.

**5. Seek Accountability**: Share your goals with a friend, mentor, or coach who can support and hold you accountable. Regular check-ins with someone can keep you motivated and on track.

**6. Practice Self-Care**: Ensure you care for your physical and mental well-being. Regular exercise, proper nutrition, and adequate sleep can enhance your energy levels and focus.

**7. Adjust as Needed**: Be flexible and open to adjusting your plan if circumstances change. It's important to adapt while still working towards your overall goal.

**8. Visualize Success**: Spend a few minutes each day visualizing achieving your goal. This can reinforce your commitment and help maintain motivation.

From time to time, reflect on what's working and what isn't. Use these insights to make necessary adjustments to your plan and approach. By implementing these strategies, you'll be better equipped to stick to the life-work revolution in the long term and stay motivated throughout the process.

## Practical Tools for Maintaining Momentum

Maintaining momentum and motivation for your long-term goals may sometimes be an uphill battle. However, integrating mindfulness and positive reinforcement into your strategy will make a difference. Let's look at how you can leverage these tools to keep your drive strong and your goals within reach.

### Mindfulness: Staying Present and Focused

Mindfulness is all about being fully present in the moment. It helps you understand your thoughts, feelings, and surroundings without judgment. When applied to goal-setting, mindfulness can improve your focus and reduce stress, making it easier to stay on track.

- **Daily Mindfulness Practice**: Incorporate a few minutes of mindfulness into your daily routine. This could be through meditation, deep breathing exercises, or simply paying attention to your thoughts and feelings. Regularly practicing mindfulness trains your mind to stay focused and grounded. This can help you better manage the ups and downs of pursuing long-term goals.
- **Set Mindful Goals**: When setting goals, be clear and specific about what you want to achieve and why. Break your long-term goals into smaller, manageable steps. This approach makes your goals feel more attainable and lets you stay mindful of each step.
- **Use Mindfulness to Manage Setbacks**: Setbacks are inevitable, but how you respond to them matters. Mindfulness can help you approach challenges with a clear and calm mindset. Instead of reacting impulsively or getting discouraged, use mindfulness to assess the situation objectively and find constructive solutions.

172

## Positive Reinforcement

Positive reinforcement involves acknowledging and rewarding your efforts and achievements. Rewards are positively associated with the behavior, increasing the likelihood of repetition. It's a powerful motivator that can keep you engaged and excited about your goals.

- **Reward Yourself Regularly**: Set up a system where you reward yourself for reaching milestones. These rewards don't have to be extravagant; even small, meaningful rewards can boost your motivation. For instance, if you complete a significant task, treat yourself to something you enjoy or take a break to relax. This creates a positive association with progress and keeps you motivated.
- **Keep a Progress Journal**: Document your achievements and progress in a journal. This can be a powerful way to reinforce your efforts. Looking back and seeing how far you've come is a tangible reminder of your capabilities and successes. This can provide a significant motivational boost, especially during challenging times.
- **Share Your Successes**: Don't hesitate to share your accomplishments with others. This doesn't mean bragging but acknowledging your progress within a supportive network. Positive reinforcement from friends, family, or colleagues can be incredibly motivating and help you stay committed to your goals.

## Combining Mindfulness and Positive Reinforcement

Integrating mindfulness with positive reinforcement can be particularly effective. Use mindfulness to stay aware of your progress and recognize moments when you've achieved something. Then, reinforce these moments by celebrating your successes. This combination ensures that you know your achievements and are motivated to continue.

Together, these strategies form a powerful toolkit for achieving long-term goals and staying motivated throughout this journey.

## Key Takeaways

- Effective habits are the cornerstone of sustained progress. Start small, be consistent, and track your progress.
- Maintaining motivation involves setting milestones, visualizing success, and staying inspired.
- Flexibility and adaptability are crucial for navigating unexpected challenges.
- Overcoming setbacks and managing stress require resilience, self-care, and support from your network.
- Sustaining progress involves continuous learning, reflection, and creating a supportive environment.

**Looking Ahead**

As we conclude our journey through the Life-Work Revolution, the final chapter will help you synthesize everything you've learned into a personalized life-work revolution strategy. It will ensure you can continue your journey towards achieving life-work synergy and creating a lasting impact.

# Chapter 17:
## Synthesizing Your Life-Work Revolution Strategy

Congratulations on reaching the final chapter of your Life-Work Revolution journey! This chapter brings everything together into a cohesive, actionable strategy to help you achieve life-work synergy and make a lasting impact. We'll revisit the key concepts, emphasize the importance of our three core pillars—Internal Revolution, External Revolution, and Community Revolution—and provide practical steps for implementing your personalized life-work revolution strategy. Let's dive in and synthesize your journey into a plan that truly works for you.

## Reaffirming the Core Pillars

As you learned in the second chapter, the Life-Work Revolution is built on three core pillars: Internal Revolution, External Revolution, and Community Revolution. Each pillar is essential for creating a balanced, fulfilling, and impactful life.

### 1. Internal Revolution
- **Focus**: Transforming your mindset, beliefs, and self-awareness.
- **Key Concepts**: Growth mindset, emotional intelligence, resilience, and self-care.
- **Action Steps**: Practice mindfulness, set clear personal goals, engage in reflective journaling, and prioritize mental and emotional well-being.

### 2. External Revolution
- **Focus**: Navigating the professional landscape, leveraging skills, and achieving career aspirations.

- **Key Concepts**: Skills inventory, dynamic career pathways, lifelong learning, and financial discipline.
- **Action Steps**: Create a comprehensive skills inventory, engage in continuous learning, diversify income streams, and develop a financial strategy for independence and legacy building.

### Community Revolution

- **Focus**: Building and leveraging supportive networks, giving back, and creating a legacy.
- **Key Concepts**: Networking, mentorship, community involvement, and legacy building.
- **Action Steps**: Join professional associations, seek mentorship, engage in community projects, and establish initiatives contributing to societal well-being.

## Synthesizing Your Strategy

Now that you understand the core pillars, it's time to synthesize them into a personalized strategy. This strategy will help you integrate your personal and professional goals, ensuring alignment with your values and aspirations.

### 1. Define Your Vision

Create a clear and compelling vision of your ideal life-work balance. Let your vision statement encapsulate your goals for personal fulfillment, professional success, and community impact.

### 2. Set SMART Actions

Establish Specific, Measurable, Achievable, Relevant, and Time-bound actions for each core pillar. Make sure each aligns with your vision.

### 3. Develop a Comprehensive Plan

Create a detailed plan that outlines the steps needed to achieve your SMART actions. Incorporate elements from the SPARC framework to set your intentions, plan your routine, act consistently, reflect on your progress, and celebrate your wins.

## 4. Leverage Your Networks

Utilize your professional and personal networks to gain support, resources, and opportunities. Map out your networks and identify key individuals who can support your journey. Engage actively and offer value to these relationships.

## 5. Implement a Financial Freedom Map

Develop financial habits and strategies that support your long-term goals and allow you to pursue your passions. Make a financial freedom map that includes budgeting, saving, investing, and income diversification. Use your high-value skills to generate additional revenue streams.

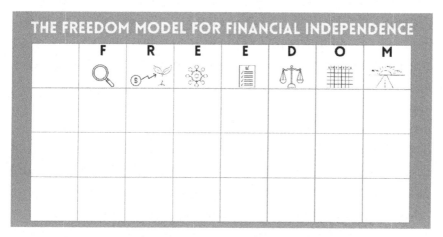

## 6. Engage in Continuous Learning and Adaptation

Commit to lifelong learning and stay adaptable to changing circumstances and opportunities. Set aside regular time for learning, experimentation, and skill development.

## Personal Examples and Reflections

I have applied these principles throughout my journey to achieve life-work synergy and create a lasting impact. Here's how these strategies have shaped my path:

**1. Internal Revolution**: I continue to work on my growth mindset—recognizing fixed beliefs and running experiments to make shifts toward growth as it relates to Health, Energy, Love, and Play to continue to optimize my day-to-day life-work synergy system.

**2. External Revolution**: I continue to leverage my skills and build my expertise to forecast and navigate the evolving workforce dynamics. I'm passionate about promoting skill-powered, tech-driven talent development and preparing organizations for unparalleled success. Through The Life-Work Revolution Book and Coaching, I fuse science-backed methods, like design and systems thinking, to facilitate transformative personal growth and skill development experiences. My coaching provides the essential tools for anyone ready to carve out fulfilling life and career pathways. I aim to grow the brand and programming to serve one million revolutionary professionals worldwide.

**3. Community Revolution**: I support projects, partnerships, and ventures that resonate with my vision of a skilled, equitable, and thriving future. My financial independence and investment strategy reflect a commitment to human innovation and lasting impact. My family organization's mission is to establish more affordable housing and life-skill programs to give back and expose others to environments and opportunities for success.

### Summing It Up

Your journey through the Life-Work Revolution has equipped you with the tools, insights, and strategies needed to create a fulfilling, balanced, and impactful life. By integrating the core pillars of

Internal Revolution, External Revolution, and Community Revolution, you can achieve life-work synergy and thrive beyond the 9-to-5. Remember, this is an ongoing journey that requires continuous learning, adaptation, and commitment. Embrace the process, stay true to your values, and enjoy the transformative journey ahead.

## Key Takeaways

- The Life-Work Revolution is built on three core pillars: Internal Revolution, External Revolution, and Community Revolution.
- Synthesizing your strategy involves defining your vision, setting SMART actions, developing a comprehensive plan, leveraging your networks, implementing a financial freedom map, and engaging in continuous learning.
- Personal examples and reflections provide practical insights into how these strategies can be applied.
- Practical exercises help you craft and implement your personalized life-work revolution strategy.

# CONCLUSION

Your journey towards life-work synergy is ongoing. It requires continuous reflection, adaptation, and commitment. Don't forget that achieving life-work synergy is impossible without financial freedom. With the FREEDOM model, you can take charge of your financial journey and your life-work revolution. The principles and strategies outlined in this book are tools to help you navigate your unique path. Each step you take is an opportunity for growth, learning, and transformation. Stay committed to your vision, embrace the process, and enjoy the journey.

Follow me on social media for daily inspiration, updates, and valuable insights. Connect with a community of like-minded individuals on their life-work revolution journey.

- **LinkedIn**: [ https://www.linkedin.com/in/kason-morris/]
- **Instagram**: [kasonmorris.official]

- **PersonalWebsite:** [https://www.kasonmorris.com/]

**The Life-Work Revolution Site**: Visit the Life-Work Revolution site [lifeworkrevolution.com] for additional resources, articles, and tools to support your ongoing journey. Engage with the community, share your experiences, and find inspiration from others navigating their life-work revolution.

If you're ready to take your life-work revolution to the next level, consider enrolling in the Life-Work Revolution coaching program. As a certified life-work design expert, I can provide personalized guidance and support to help you navigate your unique path and create a fulfilling, purpose-driven life.

**Coaching Program Includes:**

- One-on-One Coaching: Personalized sessions tailored to your specific needs and goals.
- Workshops and Webinars: Interactive sessions on design, systems thinking, and life-work synergy.
- Resources and Tools: Access to exclusive resources, templates, and tools to support your journey.
- Community Support: Join a community of like-minded individuals on their life-work revolution journey.

---

**Let's illuminate your purpose-driven path to an ideal future.** I'm here to equip you with the mindsets, tools, and skill sets necessary for living your best life and achieving your best work. Whether seeking transformation in your career, leadership development or creating more meaningful work-life integration, I offer the insight and support you need to excel.

**I invite you to connect and explore how we can collaborate on your life-work revolution.** Together, we can unlock your new possibilities and pave the way for a rewarding future. Stay connected with me via LinkedIn and the Life-Work Revolution site. Through this book and my coaching, I am here for you every step of the way.

# Last Chance to Start Your Revolution
## TODAY

Scan the QR Code Above!

# APPENDICES

## Additional Resources

### Books and Articles

- *"Atomic Habits"* by James Clear: A guide to building good habits and breaking bad ones.
- *"Grit: The Power of Passion and Perseverance"* by Angela Duckworth: Insights on the importance of grit for long-term success.
- *"The Power of Habit"* by Charles Duhigg explores the science behind habit formation.
- *"Mindset: The New Psychology of Success"* by Carol S. Dweck: Understanding the growth mindset and its impact on personal and professional development.
- *"Drive: The Surprising Truth About What Motivates Us"* by Daniel H. Pink: Insights into motivation and what drives us to achieve.
- *"Designing Your Life: How to Build a Well-Lived, Joyful Life"* by Bill Burnett and Dave Evans: Applying design thinking to life and career planning.

### Online Courses and Platforms

- **Coursera**: Offers various courses on personal development, leadership, and professional skills.
- **LinkedIn Learning**: Provides professional courses on various topics, including leadership, management, and skill development.
- **Udemy**: An extensive library of courses on personal growth, technical skills, and more.
- **edX**: Provides access to courses from top universities on various subjects.

### Podcasts

- *"The Tim Ferriss Show"*: Interviews with high-achievers across various fields.
- *"The Tony Robbins Podcast"*: Strategies and stories from leaders and entrepreneurs.
- *"Optimal Living Daily"*: Narrates the best personal development articles.
- *"The Life Coach School Podcast"*: Offers practical tools for life transformation.
- *"How I Built This"*: Stories behind the people who created some of the world's best-known companies.

**Websites and Communities**

- **Life-Work Revolution Website**: Stay updated with the latest insights, tools, and resources.
- **Medium**: Follow publications and authors who write about personal development and professional growth.
- **Reddit**: Join subreddits like r/selfimprovement and r/career to engage with like-minded individuals.
- **Life-Work Revolution Community**: Engage with a supportive community of individuals committed to their life-work revolution journey.

## Detailed Case Studies and Testimonials

### Case Study: Brandon's Journey

- **Background**: Brandon, an African American from the South Bronx, New York, faced significant socioeconomic challenges growing up. Despite these hurdles, he was determined to make something of himself.
- **Challenges**: Limited access to resources, mentorship, and opportunities. Struggles with self-doubt and finding his place in the corporate world.
- **Solution**: Under my mentorship and through the Life-Work Revolution coaching, Brandon embraced the principles of self-

184

awareness, skill-building, and networking. We worked together to identify and align his strengths with his career aspirations.

- **Results**: Brandon tripled his salary within a year, transitioned from an intern to an executive DEI consultant, and is now preparing for law school. His journey is a testament to the power of resilience, focused skill development, and leveraging community support.

## Testimonial: Brooks' Transformation

- **Background**: Brooks, an African American mid-level manager from Atlanta, Georgia, struggled to balance a demanding job and personal life. He often felt overwhelmed and stressed, leading to burnout.
- **Challenges**: High-stress work environment, lack of work-life balance, and difficulty prioritizing self-care.
- **Solution**: Through the Life-Work Revolution coaching, Brooks implemented mindfulness practices, boundary-setting techniques, and effective habit-building strategies. We focused on creating a sustainable routine aligned with his values and goals.
- **Results**: Brooks regained control over his mental health, improved his productivity, and achieved a healthier work-life balance. His morning routine now includes mindfulness meditation and exercise, significantly enhancing his overall well-being and professional performance.

## Testimonial: Reggie's Growth

- **Background**: Reggie, a Ghanaian international marketing executive from Accra, Ghana, aimed to stay ahead in his field through continuous learning and professional development.
- **Challenges**: Balancing professional responsibilities with personal growth, staying updated with industry trends, and managing work-related stress.
- **Solution**: We focused on integrating learning into Reggie's daily routine. He could stay informed without overwhelming his schedule

by reading industry-related articles and watching educational videos during his lunch breaks.

- **Results**: Reggie's knowledge and skills improved significantly, leading to career advancement and recognition within his company. His proactive approach to learning and development has made him a valuable asset and a thought leader in his field.

### Testimonial: Sarah's Transformation

- **Background**: Sarah, a first-generation Latina corporate executive from Miami, Florida, struggled with anxiety and burnout due to the high-stress nature of her job and the pressure to succeed.
- **Challenges**: Managing work-related stress, achieving a work-life balance, and maintaining mental health.
- **Solution**: Through the Life-Work Revolution coaching, Sarah implemented mindfulness practices, set clear boundaries, and prioritized self-care. We worked on building a supportive network and integrating wellness into her daily routine.
- **Results**: Sarah regained control over her mental health, improved her productivity, and enhanced her overall well-being. She now mentors other women in similar positions, sharing her journey and the tools she used to achieve a balanced and fulfilling life.

### Testimonial: Emily's Commitment

- **Background**: Emily, an engineer of Colombian heritage from Houston, Texas, wanted to incorporate regular exercise into her busy daily routine while managing her professional responsibilities.
- **Challenges**: Balancing a demanding job with personal fitness goals, finding time for self-care, and managing stress.
- **Solution**: Emily and I designed a morning routine with a yoga session right after waking up. This simple yet effective habit helped her start her day with energy and focus.
- **Results**: Emily followed this routine consistently, significantly improving her physical and mental well-being. Her commitment to self-care has enhanced her professional performance and overall

quality of life. She now advocates for wellness practices within her company, inspiring others to prioritize their health.